Scar Wars

Forged In Fright

By

J.L. Pitts

Scar Wars Forged In Fright

J.L. Pitts

Scar wars Forged In Fright
by: J.L. Pitts

Copyright © 2015 by J.L. Pitts

Published by
Christine F. Anderson Publishing & Media, Madison VA,
22727
www.publishwithcfa.com

CHRISTINE F. ANDERSON
PUBLISHING & MEDIA

ISBN: 978- 0692363058

This book is dedicated to Shirley Elems. The last conversation we had before cancer stole her from us was, "Write your book. Promise me, okay?" This is the fulfillment of that promise.

Also to my daughter Sarah who gave up a lot of mother/daughter time so I could hide out in a cabin and write this emotional tale in safety. And to Frank, my husband, who has always stood beside me.

To Stan, for providing the hideaway in the mountains where I felt safe enough to go on this emotional journey. And providing a steaming cup of cappuccino every morning.

To my father, mother, and siblings who were part of this journey and have received healing just as I did.

To God for the strength and courage and constant Presence by my side as I lived this life and healed from it and who instilled the courage in me to share so that others might also know that there is hope and healing.

Special thanks to Sandra Meeks who helped me by continually seeking out errors I had made in the first drafts.

I would like to acknowledge Beverly Engel for giving me permission to use her name and book title.

J.L. Pitts

Foreword

Judy Glaister PhD. LMFT

Sexual abuse occurs in all segments of society. Both males and females can be victims. There are many different forms of sexual abuse, ranging from suggestive remarks and fondling to sexual intercourse. The abuse can be violent and threatening to persuasive and non-menacing especially in younger children who may not understand what is happening. The perpetrators of childhood sexual abuse are often someone known to the victim. Victims of childhood sexual abuse are left with damaging consequences that can interfere with growth and development, lead to low self-esteem and relationship issues, and result in psychological impairments, such as post-traumatic stress disorder (PTSD). Survivors of childhood sexual abuse can develop PTSD because they have been faced with an event or events that threatened them and caused feelings of intense fear and helplessness. PTSD is characterized by recurrent and intrusive distressing memories of the event and persistent avoidance and numbing when confronted with these memories. Survivors often experience intense irritability and anger, hyper vigilance, difficulty concentrating, and sleep difficulties.

Julie has shared the story of her abuse and healing work. She is very brave to share with others. Healing journeys can be long and difficult and can have many obstacles, such as when Julie encountered the therapist who listened to her story and then sent her away, saying "I cannot help you." But healing is possible and healing is promoted by several factors. Having information to develop understanding of the abuse and the consequences is an important first step to healing. Next one needs to find support, someone to listen, and to guide the survivor on their journey. Finally the survivor needs to make the decision to work toward healing, to recognize and utilize their inner strengths, learn to take care of them self, challenge and find a way to come to terms with what happened to them. Healing can be impeded by other individuals who don't understand, who don't listen, who take over, who coddle, who pass out medications, or who don't encourage hard work and growth. Healing can also be impeded by activities the survivor does, such as numbing self through drinking, eating, working, or sexual activities; being negative toward oneself, being in unhealthy relationships, or by believing unrealistically that healing can occur quickly and without work or involvement on the part of the survivor.

I salute Julie and all the other survivors who have courageously worked on their healing journey and hope that if you are a survivor that you will find support and begin your healing journey soon because you are worth it.

Judy A. Glaister, PhD, LMFT

From the Author

This is an emotional journey. It is but one segment of my life. The story has very difficult parts to read, but just imagine having to live through them. There is much more to the story of my life and in time I will share those parts of the journey also. My prayer is that this book, my journey, will help another person to choose the hard road to healing, so they may have a better life to live in the future.

For every soldier that is living with and healing from Post Traumatic Stress Disorder I cannot imagine the atrocities that have put you on this journey also. But I ache in my heart that anyone suffering from any trauma has to live the kind of life that nearly ended my life so many times. For you too, there is hope and a better life waiting.

J.L. Pitts

SCAR WARS FORGED IN FRIGHT

The Beginning.

Chapter One

She was snuggled up next to her husband in bed: she was seventeen and he was twenty-one. He was her Knight in shining armor, always ready to protect her. Now the light from the street lamp had given an eerie glow to the room. She hated light creeping into a room where she was sleeping, especially when it came from behind a door jamb. She had awakened because of the moaning. *Dear God, the moaning,* she thought. It was the repetitive incessant moaning that was torturing her nightly. No one could hear it but her. She had heard it for many years yet it still frightened her. As the sun started to shine it took the place of the street lamp and when the light came through the door jamb she became extremely frightened by it. She knew her Knight would be leaving for the Army base soon and she would be all alone with the moaning. She hid under the covers so her fears did not disturb his morning routine. She never told him about hearing the moaning because they were newlyweds and she did not want him to think he had chosen what she called *damaged goods*. That thought brought back images of the miscarriage and the horror of it all made

1

her feel like something dark was lurking inside her and she just might shatter into different shards of herself. Whatever fears the night would bring, she knew she had to endure but during the day she never heard the moaning and never felt scared. That was when she changed into just another happy housewife. She would make things run smoothly in their new two bedroom trailer that had all the comforts they needed and cost all the money they could afford. She aspired to be the perfect wife and did housework, cooking, and laundry on a regular schedule. This was what she was going to be perfect at, a wife and one day a mother. She was childlike in her aspirations because truly she was only a child, but through it all she maintained a normal daytime life. It was only when the sun went down that the moaning would fill her mind and cut off all the senses, except the sense of hearing. What was it? Where did it come from? Why was it so deeply embedded in her mind? What was so wrong with those slivers of light from between the door jamb that would cause her to roll up like an infant and wish it would all go away? She was alone in this nightmarish ordeal. No one else knew the horror she endured nightly. She played the loving wife during the day and survived the nights. Her Knight in shining armor was there with her at night to make curling up like an infant feel safe. His very presence helped her through the nights when the moaning was at its worst. Even the quiet sounds from outside the house, normal night sounds, would begin to fade away until she heard nothing but the moaning in her head. Then it happened! Her Knight in shining armor had a field maneuver and would be gone for two weeks. She cried when he left, him thinking she loved him so much that parting was too hard on her, but she was thinking of the frightening nights that would come while he was away. Two weeks -- fourteen nights to get through. She put on her own mental armor and stood strong that first day. But slowly the sun sank and she did not want to go to bed. Not alone. So she stayed in the living room watching late night television until she just suddenly went to sleep. When she woke up the next morning she felt stronger and made the plan to do that for the next thirteen days. The sun would set every night and fear would grip her, but the television would keep her attention until she could just fall asleep with no sounds of moaning. It was working! Until the eighth day. She did her usual housework and then the sun took its slow time sinking into night. Somehow the darkness that came that night after the sun went down frightened her even more. The coolness of the night air made her realize fall was coming and the nights would be longer. Her heart was in her throat but she stood firm. She had the plan and it did not matter what time the sun set as long as she could just stick to the plan. She watched the late night shows, but this night was different and the moaning started before she could fall asleep. The first night since her husband -- her shield -- her Knight in shining armor had left. There was no sleeping on the couch that night because there was too much light from the streetlamp. Its eerie yellow glow made the living room, with all the windows, suddenly unfriendly. Her mind was moving fast ... what could she do to get through the night? She decided the bedroom with only one window would make things feel safer. Certainly no one would look in and with only the one window the eerie yellow light would not encompass the entire room. The thought ran through her mind, was she safe? Why had it started earlier on that night and as the very thought crossed her mind the moaning became louder than usual. She could get in the closet, but the small space would let the light in between the closet doors and that was a terrifying thought. She hid in the bed with the covers pulled all around her and that is when it happened. Her eyes were shut and she could see a room in its eerie light, but she must be dreaming because she had never seen this bedroom before, had she? The smell of bloody bandages filled the room and there lying in a hospital bed, in the dark next to the window, She could see that the man had his right leg amputated. He was the man who terrified her with his every moan., but she felt as if she was pushed further into the room by her own sisters who said she could sleep on the little bed there. When she turned around, all she could see was the light coming from the door jamb, but it was not frightening now -- it was the only way she knew others were out there while she was left with the moaning man. He was old and she had never known someone cut off. The horrifying moaning sounds were coming from him. She was still terrified and locked in this nightmarish dream world when she saw herself lay down on the nurse's cot. She could see the light through the door jamb and she kept telling herself other people were out there. She could hear her sisters laughing and playing with their two best friends in the room next to her and she remembered Mama saying that if she could not spend the night with their friends too, that they would not get to go either. So they had taken her on a long trip to the next county over where their best friends had moved and to punish her for having to come they had put her in the room with the horrible man that had no leg. His moaning seemed so tortured, it scared her. She lay there quietly listening to the moans, knowing his leg was gone. She was terrified. When the night became quiet except for the one-legged man's moan all she had was the light from the door jamb. Then slowly quietly the door had opened and there had been enough light to tell it was the father of her sister's friends. Thank God, he had come to check on her, but he was quiet and said nothing as he moved stealthily close to the cot that she lay upon. Then his cold hands touched her jeans and he was fumbling with the zipper; she did not know what was happening. Should she cry out? But a new fear rose up in her that would choke back the scream in her throat. Would that make her sisters even angrier? But really there was nothing she had the capability to do, but freeze. The father unzipped her pants and was rubbing her underwear and when he tried to take them off a clear voice rang out, "Son, what are you doing?" The man who only moaned had awakened from some dark place he was in and asked the father what he was doing. The father hastily left without saying a word. She shuddered and became aware of her own room with the eerie light and cried. The moaning she had heard all those years had deep words to them that had saved her from unknown things. She had been nine years old and after the terrifying event she had just laid there frozen in fear, going to sleep with the moaning in her ears. He had saved her. From whatever dark realm he had been in when he understood what was happening, he spoke clearly in a deep voice and saved her. She lay there in the cocoon of blankets knowing what all the fear of the lights meant and cried herself to sleep. She made it through the last days her husband was gone and the moaning in her head slowly stopped. Time froze the last night before her husband was to come home and it was like she went back in time. She remembers taking the pills. She could still taste the bitterness of all the different medications in her mouth. The torment of her small terrifying world was too much for her to bear anymore. She was just nine years old and after she took the pills she begged God to take her home to the Heaven she had learned about in Sunday School at church. She heard the voices saying, *it's okay, you need peace! Come into the void -- God will find you here and there will be no more nightmares. There will be no more pain.* She had lain down on her bed, gone into a deep sleep, and awakened in the Arms of Light. The Arms were all Light, White Pure Light! And when she looked up at the giant holding her, His face was shining so brightly she could not make an image out of it. He cradled her in the crook of his left arm and He said "Shh, it will be okay." Suddenly she was back at the edge of the void. She woke up back in her bed, feeling dizzy and sick and the first shard had been broken from within her mind.

Chapter Two

She was married to a soldier and was far away from her family, but her eighteenth birthday was coming and surely her mother would send a card with enough money that they could at least afford to get a pizza to celebrate her special day. The pay her husband brought home was barely enough to pay the bills and get a few groceries. But surely for her eighteenth birthday her mother would send money. But there were no birthday cards from anyone in the family, no calls either. They had forgotten her eighteenth birthday. There was no money for anything extra and all that marked that day was a smiley face on the calendar on the sixteenth. The day she was born. The day she just knew everyone would think of her because she had finally become a grown up No one treated her like she was a grown up when she married at seventeen. But now they just had to because she was eighteen! Her husband came home that night, whisked her around, looked into her deep blue eyes, and asked, "how does it feel to be a grown up?" But she just laid her head on his strong shoulder and cried because really at eighteen she was not truly a grown up then either. She was childlike in her thinking and childlike in her attitude towards life. It was just another day that came and went. Her husband was stationed at Fort Bragg, North Carolina and he always had to leave really early in the morning for P.T. She had learned when they first met that the letters stood for *Physical Training*, but what they actually did was run.

They ran five miles every day except on Fridays when they ran ten. Her husband was in the best shape of his life when he turned twenty-two. Just sixteen days after she had turned eighteen. There was no extra money for his birthday either. But she had secretly slipped into the groceries that week a chocolate cake mix and a can of chocolate frosting, which were his favorite. When his birthday arrived, she took the cake mix out and got ready to bake it when she realized she had no baking pan. She did not even have cupcake tins. Thinking about her neighbor, a sweet German woman, she mustered up enough courage and went and asked if she could borrow a pan to bake the cake in, explaining her dilemma. The woman was very kind to her and in her thick German accent invited her in and that was when she saw the prettiest little boy she had ever seen. They were introduced and the little boy just made her feel giggly inside. Even though she and her husband kept trying ever since the miscarriage, she had not been able to conceive. Now here was this little boy with blue eyes that were so bright blue they actually seemed to sparkle. The German woman gave her the pan and said she could keep it. She was so grateful she told her if she ever needed a babysitter she would repay her kindness with pleasure. Then she proceeded to go back to her trailer and made her cake. When her husband came home he could not believe she had made him his favorite cake. He smothered her with kisses that turned into long passionate ones until she pulled herself away and told him that she had made dinner and after that he could have cake. They ate and talked about his long work day and when he was ready for cake he saw that she had drawn "Happy

Birthday" in the frosting. He grabbed her and said "You are the best!" She looked him squarely in the eyes and told him that everyone should get a cake on their birthday and he swallowed hard. He remembered that for her birthday there was no cake and they only had hot dogs for dinner that night. She explained to him that when she was little her birthday came right before school started. Because there were seven children to get ready for school, they always went school shopping and each child would get three pairs of pants and five shirts. She always got her new things wrapped up like birthday gifts, and it burned in her heart that nothing special was given to her. Only one thing was different, her mother would always bake her favorite cake -- Cherry Chip with white icing. Her sisters and her brothers would beg her to pick chocolate because that was what they liked, but she would always say she wanted the Cherry Chip cake with white icing and her mother would always make it. That was what separated her birthday from back-to-school shopping. That was when he saw from the look in her eyes that birthdays were special to her and he never forgot that lesson in love again.

The holiday season arrived pretty quickly. They had pizza for Thanksgiving dinner and ate the whole thing together. Then they snuggled up in bed and were happy they could afford a pizza to make the day special. Christmas was coming next, but they didn't talk about it because they both knew there was no extra money in the budget to make it special. Then one day when she was particularly lonely, a quiet little knock came upon her door and it was the beautiful little boy from next door. He was only three and shouldn't have been outside by himself. She invited him in and gave him a cup of hot chocolate to drink. Then gently taking his hand, she walked him back home. She had to keep knocking loudly in order for his mother to hear. The sweet German woman came to the door with sleep still in her eyes and was horrified to see her little boy outside with her next door neighbor. She explained quickly that he had come to her house and she gave him a cup of hot chocolate to drink and brought him right home. The woman started to cry, thanking her all the while. She started explaining how she had been working double shifts and her babysitter had quit on her. The sweet German lady was crying as the words tumbled out of her. It was like it had been so long since she had a friend to talk to about things. She reminded her neighbor that she had offered to babysit when she asked to borrow the cake pan. She told the woman not to worry anymore, that her problem was solved and so she could relax and get some sleep. The woman looked deep into her eyes and said today was just one day -- what would she do for the rest of the days, weeks, months? She excitedly told her neighbor she would babysit for as long as she needed her. The woman looked her in the eyes and said it was long hours but that she could pay her very well. The new little wife that couldn't get pregnant excitedly told her she did not mind at all. She went on to tell the neighbor she needed the money because Christmas was coming. Besides she just she adored the little boy. On that day both women's needs were met. The German woman found somebody to trust to keep her child and the new little wife would finally have a child in her life and extra money for Christmas.

They went on like that for a few months. Christmas

had been better because of the money she had made babysitting. Things weren't so tight and they could afford a few more groceries and pizza on Friday nights. But what she really liked was that her maternal instincts were being fed. Then one day her husband came home and told her he had orders from the Army and they had to move. At first she was excited and danced around the living room until she saw the sadness in his face. "What is wrong?" she asked.

He lowered his head and could not look in her eyes as he said, "It is called a single man's tour".

She stopped and looked at him with fear in her eyes. "What does that mean?"

Then she heard him say words that seemed to make the world come crashing down around her. "I have to go to Korea for twelve months and you cannot come".

She actually began to shake and asked, "Can I stay here and wait on you to come home back home?" He told her they would not have the money to support a household in America while he had to go to a foreign country that he did not know anything about and still have money to live on. But where would she go? There was only one answer and it hit her like a bullet but she asked anyway, "But where will I go?"

He said, with a tremble of fear in his voice, the words that seemed like a prison sentence. "You have to go back to your family". And then she saw the little blond haired girl with the sad frightened look in her deep blue eyes holding up her bloody hands and asking, "What does it mean"? She knew that she had seen that frightened little girl before.

J.L. Pitts

Chapter Three

She had escaped from home when she ran away at seventeen. She had run away because she had been raped by a family member who was held in such high esteem that she knew no one would believe her. Somehow she knew something bad was going to happen that day when her mother announced she and their father had to do some business in Ocala, Florida where her mother's sister lived. That since it was business they were only taking the three youngest of the seven children. She begged her mom to let her stay at home by herself, but her parents hated her boyfriend. They were afraid she would take advantage of the situation and use the time to be intimate since there was no one around to chaperone. She tried to comfort herself that she would be with other loving family members, her older brother, her sister, her brother-in-law, and their precious little baby boy. He was the first grandchild and her only nephew and he was not quite a year old yet. She just felt as if she was in some kind of danger but she did not know why. It flooded her mind with fear to be left with family rather than to stay alone way out in the country where their house was located. When her mother and father took them to her eldest sister's house she was extremely angry with both of them. Her sister and brother-in-law thought it was time to celebrate when her parents left, broke out the beer and marijuana, and everyone got drunk and high. She had the strange thought that she had tasted beer and smelled marijuana before. She

12

suddenly became scared just being at her sister's house. For some reason, the thought went through her head that there was safety in numbers and she knew she would be okay. Then her older brother's allergies took over and in seconds his airway was closing. They realized there was no time to wait for an ambulance! Her sister took her brother, who was drunk and high and whose airways were closing up, to the local emergency room to get him immediate help. Maybe this was what the feeling of being in danger she had felt was all about. She thought that the feeling of being in danger was just because they had been partying and her brother had gotten sick. They waited diligently to hear news from the hospital. For some reason it felt like a death sentence to the sixteen year old when her sister called to say he was in serious condition. That she would not be back because she could not leave him alone like that. It was late when they got the news so she fixed a place on the couch to go to sleep and her brother-in-law told her to go back to their room and sleep with the baby. She thought that was a good idea and went to lay down beside her sleeping nephew. Because of all the drugs and alcohol she had consumed, she passed out very quickly. Then the events that took place next were nightmarish and changed her life forever.

The brother-in-law came into the room and took the sleeping baby from beside her. In her dazed and drugged stupor, she thought he did that because he was afraid she would roll over on the baby and smother him. She passed out again, deeper now that the baby was gone because she didn't have to be on alert in case he woke up in the night. Deeper, deeper, and she woke up with someone inside her body! The back door! Did she lock the back door? It was such a bad neighborhood! Who was raping her? And then she looked in the face of the man that was raping her and it was her brother-in-law. "Get off me!" she screamed. Obscenities flew through her mind and immediately out of her mouth. He would not remove himself from her body and so she started saying things to shame him to make him feel like he was inept and worthless. Finally her got off her and left the room. She quickly got up, redressed herself, and left the trailer through the back door even though it was in the middle of the night. Her mind was wild with all the thoughts running around. *He had raped her!* Should she call the police? No, they would blame her because she had been in his bed, drugged up. Or maybe they would say it was a just a mistake he had made because he had been noted in the newspaper as the county's very own tennis champion. She knew the small town police would protect him and his reputation. She quickly realized that was not even an avenue she could choose. She could tell her sister! *No, no, no!* That would devastate her -- he was her whole world! She could tell her mother and father when they came back, but she knew no one would believe her.

He was treated like he was the greatest thing that happened to their family in a long time. He was a hard worker and always helped her parents in any way he could. He was always buying goodies for the younger children that rarely came their way since they were poor. He would come to pick up her sister for a date and stay and have quality family time. He was the perfect gentleman.

She thought since she was fat that no one would

believe he had any interest in her especially since her sister was so slim and beautiful. She felt she was nothing in the family's eye since she had been a bed wetter and sucked her thumb until she was thirteen. She felt no one in the family spoke any kind words to her unless they wanted her to pray for them because she was the only one who stayed in church. She just knew no one would ever believe her. She would just make the family mad at her and all she knew to do was keep quiet and never be alone with him again.

She walked until daylight and when she thought for sure he would not be awake, she went back to the trailer. She prayed he was not waiting on her. She entered the trailer the same way she had left and saw that he had gone into his room and shut the door. Then she heard the baby stirring and went to take care of his needs. All the while she wondered what should she do. She decided to leave home and run away so he could never get his hands on her again. There was no one she could tell! No one would believe her and if they did believe, they would say she ruined everything! No one would believe her because she had always been a ghost in the family and to them he was the epitome of what family stood for.

It seemed like an eternity until her sister and brother came home from the hospital. So the ghost of a girl created the plan to save up the money she made from babysitting and run away to New York City. She planned to be gone before the beginning of her senior year in high school. She would get everything ready so she could leave. Then unfortunately her mother found the stash of money and thought it was for school clothes and told her for her birthday she would take her shopping for new clothes. Her plan was ruined!

She decided to call a good friend who was stationed in Fort Hood, Texas in the Army and tell her everything that had happened. How her mother had found out about the money and how now she had to use it on clothes for school. Right then and there, she hatched a new plan. She would go ahead and get the clothes, but save some money back and ask another friend to make up a story about how her family was going shopping in the big city nearest to the small town where they lived. How she wanted to take her with her family, that they would get to stay in a hotel, and that she would only be gone for three days. Her mother bought the story and gave her blessing.

She only had three days to get to Texas. The next thing she had to work out was more difficult. She needed a safe grown up to tell the story to and get their advice on what to do next. She picked her favorite teacher from high school who had always been on the underdog's side, The teacher informed her former student that it would cause her to lose her teaching license if anyone ever found out The teacher helped her anyway because just hearing about what had happened to her former student gave her the resolve to help.

Her teacher and her friend in the Army got enough money together so she could buy a bus ticket to get to Killeen, Texas, the town where her friend was stationed. The only other thing she needed was someone to get her to the closest bus station, but one that wouldn't be searched if it was found out she had actually run away. She had the perfect friend for that. He had called her "Bubbles" when he came into her life because of how happy she seemed at her new job as a cashier at a burger joint. He was a regular

16

customer and she always had a smile for him and he always had a joke for her. She really hated the job and was glad when the burger chain was bought out by a new franchise. She had remained friends with the nice, little old man and that gave her the courage to ask him to help. He was hesitant until she told him everything she had been living through since she was a child. He also knew the girl's fiancé and did not like him at all. He decided that getting her away from that scoundrel and the horrible living conditions would be the best thing for her. He also joined the pact and everything was settled.

That is just how the plan worked out. It was executed silently and quickly and when she reached Houston, Texas, she called the runaway hotline. She asked them to tell her mother that she was in Texas. There was a letter in the top dresser drawer for her and that the letter would explain everything. Finally, she made it to Killeen, Texas. No one had stopped her on the bus trip. All the fear she had felt drained from her body and she felt ready to collapse. She had to keep going though because she still had to make her way through the bus station to find her friend and her friend's husband who were waiting to pick her up. They finally found each other and headed back to where the newlyweds lived.

There turned out to be a lot of people there. All of them were drinking, but she didn't dare. She was too afraid to get drunk around men especially since they were ones she didn't know. Then she saw him ... she knew right at first sight he would be her husband one day. He was coming in her friend's front door when their eyes met. It was love at first sight. She subtly let him know right away that he was the one she wanted to be with even though there were other soldiers at the house. Maybe love was blind because she saw none of his flaws when she met him. What she did see was he had the most beautiful face and she knew that the beauty went right down to his soul.

They saw each other every day but he was dependent on other people for rides from the base to the trailer park where she was living with her friend. He had just wrecked his car and it had been totaled. It worked out anyway because a lot of people in his unit lived in that area and they would just bring him from the base when they were on their way home. Then came a day when he could not find a ride. He was not going to be able to come that day and it hurt her heart. She started cleaning and doing laundry because that is how she paid her friend to stay there. She had agreed to become their live-in maid.

She was just finishing folding the laundry when there was a knock at the front door. She was not expecting anyone so she thought it must be the nosy neighbors. When she opened the door there he stood with flowers in his hands. She knew she would love him forever because he had just walked the seven miles from the Army base all the while picking wild daisies for her. When he got inside the door and gave her the flowers, she knew -- they both knew -- that they would stay together forever. That afternoon they walked up the hill next to the trailer park and sat down to watch the sunset. He suddenly turned to her and said that if he asked her to marry him, would she be willing to go back to his hometown in Georgia. She told him she would go anywhere in the world in order to marry him! From that day forward they would only spend two months apart until they were married.

Chapter Four

The two month separation happened when she went home to her family to get married. They were getting ready for the wedding she never wanted. She just wanted to go before a judge and do paperwork and be married, but her mother had to sign for her to get married at seventeen and had insisted she come back home to Florida where they would have a real wedding. Meanwhile, her soon-to-be husband's enlistment in the Army was finished. He went to Georgia and got a job in his hometown.. They could only wait for the wedding date that her mother had set. She stayed at her mother's house. Her mother had told her she could get married any time after May first. She asked why it had to be after that day and her mother told her a secret that none of the other children knew. The first five children she had given birth to belonged to her first husband, but all the children knew that. Then she told her daughter about the Social Security money that came every month for the children because he had died. That she had applied for benefits for the children and every month since his death she had received a check for the kids. Right then she was using the money to pay off her car and May 1st would be the earliest she could give up those benefits. She would have to wait until the end of the summer to get married *without permission*, but if she let her mother keep the secret money for just two more months she would sign for her to get married before her eighteenth birthday.

It was the only choice she had: she could not go and live with her husband-to-be because that would have upset his dad who was a devoted Christian. This was the only way she could get married early. So she took the deal and decided to wait out the two months. It was horrible being there with everyone looking at her and wondering why she ran away. Wondering if she was pregnant because she was heavier now than when she first ran away. Pregnant?

She was not pregnant but she wished with all her heart that she had her future husband's baby inside her. It was like her mother knew what she was thinking. One day her mother said for her wedding gift she was taking her to the doctor and getting her on the pill. They went to the doctor together and her mother was behind her in the examining room. She hovered and looked at the doctor and when the doctor told her when to start the pill she felt all the tension in her mother's body drain away. She knew her mother just wanted to know if she was pregnant. Now her mother knew that she didn't *have* to get married that she really did love this young man.

That was when she saw the little girl with the blond hair and deep blue eyes holding up her bloody hands as if asking what it meant. It was the first time the girl had appeared in her mind. It was so shocking she didn't know that they were in the car driving to the drugstore to get the birth control pills. It was her mother's idea not hers.

Ever since she had miscarried his baby in Texas she knew she wanted to have his children right away. Here she was being given a pill to take and given directions to take it every day at the same time and not to miss one and that way she would not get pregnant. She took the pills in her hand knowing that taking them was not what she wanted and even though it was a small pill she choked it down to hide a sob. She took the pills, hid them, and did not take another one until her mother found out. Her mother made her take all the pills she had missed at one time and told her *she would not get pregnant!* That's when she started getting a glass of tea carefully every morning and went to the bathroom to take her pill. She took the pill out of its wrapper, dropped it down the drain, drank the tea, and left the pill case on the counter to be a sign that she was taking the pill everyday right at the same time.

The wedding would have to be very simple because there had never been any money ever set aside for weddings or even college. She again asked her mother to just let them go in front of a judge and get married in the courthouse, but her mother would not have it. Then her mother set the whole wedding up and the only thing the girl got to choose was the colors. Her mother informed her she was going to wear a white dress and a friend of the family was going to make it for her. That person just happened to be her eldest sister's mother-in-law.

The mother of the man that raped her.

The woman asked what kind of material the girl wanted it to be made from and she immediately said white eyelet. Her dream dress would have a sweet heart neckline and would be so long it would touch the floor with a small train behind, but the sister's mother-in-law convinced her to make it a street length dress so she could wear it again. Having no real control, she went to the fittings with her best friend for comfort and courage. She needed the support because after every fitting she saw the little blond haired girl with the sad deep blue eyes on a bed holding her bloody hands up wanting to know what it meant. Finally the dress was done. She looked in the mirror and all she could see in her own eyes was the white eyelet material and the sweetheart neckline and she was happy. She was also happy that she would not have to see her sister's mother-in-law again. She took the dress home and her mother approved. She placed it in the closet along with the veil the woman had made to match the dress. Suddenly she was glad that if her mother was going to *make* her have a wedding that she had the white eyelet dress and veil to wear in front of all those people her mother had invited.

On the first Friday after the first day of May, she stood before all those people in her mother's living room with her beloved groom and recited her vows. He then recited his vows to her. She could tell it was forever for him because his voice was full of deep emotion and a tear slid down his face. Rings were placed on fingers, papers were signed. And that was when she saw what her sister's mother-in-law was wearing. It was a simple house dress but without a sweetheart neckline and in a colorful pattern. Her white eyelet dress with the sweetheart neckline was just a house dress changed just enough so that people would look at it differently. Her best friend stood beside her as her maid of honor and understood the horrified look on her face because she had noticed the same thing.

She was told they needed a picture of her with her bouquet, which was made with tea daisies -- the closest thing to the flowers he had picked for her on the long journey from the Army base to where she lived in Killeen. She was happy about that part of the wedding and then the cake was cut and pictures were taken of the two newlyweds feeding it to each other. There were all kinds of foods set out in buffet style dishes. All that mattered to the girl was that they were now married and she was free!

She left the guests to stay for the small wedding reception that was also held in her mother's house. She got in the car with her new husband and went to the steakhouse down the road. She sat in her frock of a wedding dress with the veil still swung back from when her beloved had uncovered her face. That is where they chose to have their wedding dinner -- away from her controlling mother, her rapist and his mother who had tricked her into a modified house dress to wear as her wedding gown. Then they went to the nicest motel in the area and consummated their love as a legally married couple. She hoped that her wedding night would be the night that she would get pregnant and her maternal instincts would be fulfilled.

The next day, the girl went back to her mother's house picked up the things she had packed the day before. She kissed and hugged her large family goodbye and started on a journey that would take her life on a wild spin around the world Suddenly she saw her again: the little girl sitting on the bed. Beads of sweat appeared on her forehead. Her hands were outstretched with the blood on them and she asked with her eyes what did the blood mean, could she help her. The new bride just shook the picture out of her head.

She went back to her husband's hometown to find out that the foreman had fired him because he had taken off for the wedding and honeymoon. He had only missed four days. The foreman said her husband had missed too many days in his probationary period. He explained to the manager of the company that he had to go to Florida for his wedding when he interviewed for the job and the manager approved the time off. However, the foreman still fired him.

They had an apartment, they had a little food, and she was afraid that there was no way they could make it in the civilian world. The only job he could get to keep them from sinking was as a fry cook at a coffee shop. On the day she took off her wedding ring -- the simple gold band that was to remind them to keep it simple -- and pawned it for ten dollars to get money for food, they knew he would have to return to the military life.

Chapter Five

So there she stood in her living room with her husband's boyish face clouded with tears telling her he had six months before he would be transferred from Ft. Bragg Army Base to a base in South Korea and that he couldn't take her with him. He was telling her that one month after their first wedding anniversary he would be leaving her for twelve months.

Five months flew by and on their first anniversary at the beginning of May, they went back to her parents' house. Fortunately for them her husband had been given travel time by the Army. Thirty paid vacation days for relocating his household and family to a new area. Usually this meant finding housing, turning on utilities, and packing or unpacking things that were in military storage. For them it only meant packing the few things they had in the back of their *new* used, white pick-up truck and heading back to her mother's house. The journey took thirteen hours but seemed to go by really fast. Somehow in a horrid twist of fate she had to return home where she had started from and she would only get to spend twenty days with her husband. He would use the other ten days for travel time to South Korea, being assigned to a new unit, getting his new gear, and settling in a new room in the barracks. The twenty days went by and the couple was treated as man and wife. The girl thought finally after turning eighteen and being married for a year her mother and father would look at her as an adult and at first they did.

Until her husband flew out for Korea and then she was given restrictions on how she would live under their roof. There were curfews, chores, and giving them money so she could say she was not there rent-free. Her misery caused from being back home had just begun.

On the ninth day after her husband reached his base in South Korea, he sent her nine yellow roses. The card that accompanied the flowers had just three words, *I miss you!* He called using a phone card to see if she got them and she said they were beautiful and it was wonderful that he had sent nine roses on the ninth day he was gone. He said that he had only paid for six, but maybe somehow God knew it should nine! There they were, the nine yellow roses to show for each one of the days he had been gone. He told her that she would always be his yellow rose of Texas. He had half of his check sent to his wife and she paid on the bills they had accumulated.

Her mother told her she still needed to get a job. So she got a job taking care of a mentally challenged young man. He was very childlike and the interaction between them fed her maternal instincts. She loved her job and the sweetness between them made his family happy to have her as his caretaker.

She got a call from her husband. He told her some of the Army wives got visitors' visas and were actually living in South Korea with their husbands. There were apartments to rent off-base and if they could get her a passport and visa, she could come live with him in South Korea. She spoke with the family that she was working for as caretaker. She explained with much regret that she needed to get a higher paying job so she could join her husband in South Korea.

She found a job at a convenience store where the manager happened to be the mother of the three little girls she had babysat in her younger teenage years. It worked out that she could work the shift opposite of her manager's and could babysit the manager's three little girls for extra money. She felt the real bonus was that it also fed her maternal instincts. Along with her pay from the convenience store, the babysitting money, and the allowance her husband gave her out of his pay, she paid off all their accumulated bills.

She then started saving for the passport and visa. That was the hardest thing she had to do. She had to go to the Korean Consulate in the largest city nearest to her and ask for a six month visitor's visa. She was frightened and felt childlike, but she handled it as if she was an experienced traveler. The only other thing she had to do was keep working and get the money for the flight. It cost twelve hundred dollars just to fly from Atlanta International Airport to San Francisco and then on to South Korea. It would be the first flight that she ever took and it would take four hours from Atlanta to San Francisco, and then on to the Korean Airlines where she would travel over ten hours on a flight to South Korea.

She boarded the plane looking good, feeling grown-up and accomplished. But the little girl inside her was scared that the plane would crash. She sat by the window to watch the plane take off from the runway and fly like a giant bird into the air. She just knew it was going to be a wonderful flight but she immediately got dizzy and sick to her stomach. She asked the stewardess for help, but was told they could not dispense any medications. She felt the next four hours were the longest she had ever known. She was as sick as she could be. The stewardess told her when she got to San Francisco there would be shops where she could buy a product that would ease the airsickness. She quickly wrote the name down as if just knowing the name of the medicine would give her some relief. Finally, she watched the plane descend onto the runway and knew that once she disembarked from this plane, bought the airsickness medicine, and got to her next flight and all would be okay.

Coming around the bend of the walkway of the plane, she walked into the busiest place she had ever been to in all her life! All kinds of people from all kinds of different countries were hurrying about, going on their own journeys. She finally found someone to help her find out how to get to her next flight. They simply remarked that she needed to go to the international side of the airport and would have to take a tram to get there. Another person showed her where to wait for the next tram. She had less than twenty minutes to get to the international side and be at the gate before her plane took off.

She watched as she passed stores but had no time to stop and get the medicine for airsickness. But she reasoned that surely they would have some stores at the International departure gates and she would buy some there. She quickly found the right tram and sat down as if she were in a puddle. She felt very grown up and very little at the same time. She then steeled herself and sat up, looking like a young woman that was used to flying on international flights.

When they arrived at the gates she left the tram and started running through the gateways searching signs for the gate she was supposed to depart from. She finally found her gate and was ten minutes early. She started looking for stores where she could buy the airsickness medicine, but all she could see were row upon row of gates. The man at the entrance to the international flights had told her once she passed his checkpoint she was not be able to go back to the stateside terminal but that didn't matter. She would find her a store and everything would be fine. Unfortunately she found out there were no stores on the international departure side.

She found her way back to her gate and melted into the hard plastic chair, no longer worried if she looked childlike because that's exactly the way she felt: like a child stuck in a nightmare. She would have to fly over ten hours feeling airsick and there was nothing she could do about it. They called for people to board the plane. She stood in line with her ticket and was finally allowed to board since all her paperwork was in order. She walked the long archway to the plane in awe. This plane was so much bigger than the first plane and it frightened her all the more. She sat in a window seat and watched the plane lift off the runway. The horrid airsickness came back but she mercifully fell asleep.

Chapter Six

When she finally woke up they were moving into their final descent. She was still airsick but it was almost over. The stewardess handed her a form to fill out about any monies, jewelry, or high-priced items she might be bringing into South Korea and she was very confused. All she had was a twenty-five dollar watch and a wedding ring that had been bought for thirty dollars. She read the paper carefully and found where it indicated that if her items were valued at less than five hundred dollars she did not have to disclose them. Thank goodness for that, since she really did not know how to fill out the paperwork anyway.

When she departed the plane, she started looking for her luggage right away. Her bags were right there, already waiting on her. She retrieved them and waited in line to go through customs. The pace was very frenzied and they were suddenly opening her suitcase and travel trunk. They hurriedly went through everything and she blushed red because they were touching all of her private things. She watched as they frantically went through her clothes, her undergarments, and everyone else could see her private belongings. She was thankful it was a fast process. She showed her passport with the visa and was finally let through Customs. That was when she saw the dirty little blond haired girl with scars all over her and as fast as she had caught the glimpse of her she was gone. She had not seen the girl in the living world but had only seen the child in her mind. Right now she was too distracted to ponder a glimpse of a dirty, little, scarred-up, blond headed girl that was revealing herself in her mind!

She was desperately looking through the sea of people, all with dark hair, moving and shoving her forward. Where was her husband and how could she find him with all these dark haired people pushing her about?

Then she saw him -- her husband, her beloved. She saw that beautiful face that carried beauty all the way down to his soul. He grabbed her and swung her around and she gripped him tightly as if she would have let go he would vanish. The beginning of the real journey was just about to begin. Hurriedly he grabbed her bags and swiftly maneuvered her through the throng of dark haired people. He looked to find the right bus and they were off.

The airsickness had finally faded away but suddenly fear gripped her when she realized she was very far away from America. That thought squelched all sounds, sights, and smells that were quickly passing by outside of the bus window. Finally they reached a building with an apartment in it where she could sit down and relax. And she cried. She had accomplished the greatest journey she had ever been on in her entire life and now she was finally with him again. He introduced her to two Korean girls who barely spoke English but somehow they worked together to show where she would sleep and that the mat on the kitchen floor was where to eat. They showed her a bathroom with a shower and then they showed her the strangest of things. It was round and tall and had holes in top of it and no matter how hard they tried to explain this round black thing with holes she did not understand what it was. She did find out that if she touched the thing it left black smudges on her fingers.

Her husband came and explained that everything that needed warm water - - the shower, the kitchen, and the heating system below the floors - was fueled by coal. He took her to a bin, opened it, and she could see the coal burning red at the bottom of the round cylinders carefully placed in a row. The house was warm and she was invited to take a shower, which she welcomed with pure joy.

After she showered, she had to dig through her luggage for clean clothes. . Her things were hard to find because the frenzied hands of the customs agents had made a mess in the suitcase and travel trunk. She lay down on the mat and her husband covered her with a thick heavenly feeling blanket and she slept.

When she woke up, the two Korean girls were talking in a funny broken sort of English and told her that "her husband had to go to work now". She was quite frightened because she had only known these girls for less than four hours and if she counted the almost three and a half hour nap, she had not known them long at all. But they talked softly in their broken English and patted a space to come sit near them. They told her their names. The curly haired girl spoke first and told her an Asian name she had to learn to pronounce. The girl with the long straight jet black hair, who happened to speak the most English, spoke last. She had an American name and never went by her Korean name now that she was engaged to a soldier. They tried to tell her about many things, so many things they all got jumbled up in her head and seemed unreal.

Finally, mercifully her husband came home with some food and she ate her first Korean meal. It was fried rice with egg and vegetables in it. She was famished and ate all of hers and part of his and as he had always done he saved his last bite for her. He took her outside into this world that seemed imaginary. She had never seen a third world country except on television. The first thing that hit her was the smell, which consisted of so many things she stopped her husband from telling her any more about the meat markets and fish markets because the smell of it all made her think she might get sick.

He walked her down a long road of buildings which were all bars. He walked her around the block and she found out the blanket she loved was called a *double mink blanket*. He showed her where he had bought it and there, with blankets fixed like a house all around her, was a wrinkled old woman with gray in her black hair yelling something in Korean. Her husband just lifted his hand and said not today. He brought her all the way around the whole city block and on the other end there were no bars. On that end there were food stands with the Koreans hastily yelling out in broken English "come eat good food". She was thankful for this part of the walk because the wonderful food smells drowned out the horrid smell that was Seoul, Korea.

They were in a little suburb of the giant city of Seoul. All the suburbs seemed to just melt into the big city. Theirs was a little village inside the suburb and it was quiet except for the vendors calling out in broken English, "Now you come buy" or "blanket good for you." All the vendors knew different phrases and peddled what they were selling to anyone who stopped. The only thing they had in common was one word that they said twice in a row "cheap, cheap". There was also "I give you good price" and "you buy here." It was a world she never imagined existed. But here she was in a third world country sticking out as a blond haired, blue eyed woman in a sea of dark haired, dark eyed, and bronze skin people.

Suddenly, it was all too much and that feeling of being a small child came over her, so she asked to go back to the apartment. Once there, they realized they were alone. However, they still did not make love because of the chance someone would come in. He explained this was not the house they would live in and that he was trying to find them a smaller apartment that they could afford. That is when he took her hands in his and told her he had to leave the village and the base to go down to a far southern region of South Korea to a place called Cheju Do and would be away a week.

The girls came back with two soldiers who looked quite at home when they came through the door and she automatically knew this was their place. She was to stay there with the two girls while he was gone to Cheju Do. He said when he got back, he would find a place they could afford and they would move into their own home. The other soldiers were also going on the mission to learn how to repel down the sides of mountains. They left the next day leaving her with the curly haired girl and the girl who had the long straight jet black hair. The only food she would eat was the white rice they made in a big pot. They offered her other foods but she did not know what kind of food it was. That whole first week all they could get her to eat was white rice.

Chapter Seven

Her husband left her money that was strange and funny looking. The first night that the guys were gone the two Korean girls told her they were going to a party and she should come too. All this was in broken English. But she dressed up in nice clothes, fixed her hair and make-up, and went outside into that big, foreboding world that was nothing like America. She followed the two girls down a street to a bar that they called a club. Inside they were playing songs so loud she could hardly make them out but finally recognized them as songs that had been popular years before in America. It was so loud and there were so many flashing lights she felt dazed and confused. She was asked to dance a few times but was too shy to go with them. The girls had bought her a cola that didn't taste like any cola she had ever had. It was quite bad, tasting more like seltzer water than cola. But the girls got braver and introduced her to a peach wine called Oscar. It tasted so good, like a peach straight from the tree. The unsuspecting girl drank a lot of the peach wine and this time when men asked her to dance she went with them. At about 4:00 o'clock in the morning everything shut down like a strange carnival done for the night. She went home with the two girls, laid down with her double mink blanket, and really just passed out.

The next day she ate white rice for breakfast and lunch. The Korean girls just laughed at her and offered her different foods that did not look like any food she had ever seen. She politely refused it and stayed strictly with the white rice. They realized she had never gone to *a party* -- as in partying at a club -- before in her life. She was only eighteen and she could not drink in America but here there seemed to be no age limit. Here in Korea there seemed to be no limits at all. The next the day she ate white rice for breakfast and lunch and at night she went to different clubs. She felt like she had stepped through some sort of mangled looking glass. Finally, they came to one little bar that had soft music. It had no bright flashing lights, and only a few people and she liked that. The curly haired Korean loved the place but the straight haired girl did not care for it and decided to go home. The bar looked as if it were the inside of a red velvet cake. Everything was red velvet, even the walls. The two drank the peach wine and at closing time they went home as fast as they could through the darkened streets. They got back to the nice apartment, fell asleep under double mink blankets, and slept until late afternoon.

Every day when they got up, she would refuse any new "food" and only eat white rice for breakfast and lunch. And each night around sunset they fixed themselves up, and went back to the "party". The curly haired girl soon realized that this American they had taken under their wing was emotionally exhausted. She took her back to the red velvet bar that was quiet and simple with not too many people coming inside. She drank the peach wine and when she was offered a cigarette she took it and it was the first of many she would smoke for the next ten years. Thankfully this was the last night before her husband would come home. She just thought this lifestyle was just something the girls did because they were alone for the week. That last night she laid down her head and thanked God her husband would be home to save her. He came back all cleaned up, dressed in nice new clothes and looking really good. Technically he still lived on the base and that was where all his things remained. His commander had given him time off to find a place to live. He did not make much money and was still paying for his truck back home, which meant money was tight. Their budget limited them from finding really nice apartments but as long as they would be together they thought everything would turn out all right.

One morning he took her to this little place where there was a gate that enclosed a very small courtyard. He brought her inside and there stood a short gray haired old woman and she eyed them warily. He then said some Korean words to her and she showed him to a door. She said "you take shoes off" in broken English. They did and placed them on a shelf that held other people's shoes as well. The woman stepped up on a wooden platform and waved them past the first door into the second, behind which was a very small room with a double sized bed that was just a stuffed hard packed mattress on the floor. That was the room they would live in -- one room. She took them to the back wall and it was made out of some flimsy wood and parchment paper. She carefully pushed it aside and showed them the *kitchen*. It was a small block of concrete and underneath the lid there was a round coal block that was ready to be lit. Now the girl thought *I am definitely in a third world country*. She went back out of the *apartment* and the old lady took them around her own house into a big bathroom that was very cold. She then explained in broken English that this was a bathroom for everyone in the apartments. It was like living hundreds of years ago. That's where they would have to live but they were happy to be together.

For entertainment they would go down the hill to the red velvet bar. The owner became very good friends with her husband and it seemed to be a safe place. One night they went to the red velvet bar and she saw an older white male with a small Korean boy. She was shocked and thought the boy was in trouble so she went to the table and confronted the man. He laughed and said that he was working here in South Korea as part of his mission studies as a new priest. The boy seemed happy and she was introduced to him and given his name. The priest, who would become a devoted friend, invited her to join them. She sat there and enjoyed talking with them the rest of the night. The priest was trying to get the boy into a trade school and the boy was adamant about not going. He left her and the priest to talk. "Where does he live?" she asked the priest.

He replied that the boy lived on the street in a matter of fact way. She found out that the boy's family had kicked him out when he was five because they had too many mouths to feed. His older sisters were sold into prostitution and part of their earnings went back to their parents on a monthly basis.

She tried to listen to the priest but was seeing the little girl with ragged, dirty, blond hair peeking and scars on her body behind a large object but she was not clear what it was. She could see the little girl vividly, but not the object in front of her. The small Korean boy had scars, real scars all the way down his left side. Maybe that's why the dirty, scarred, little girl had peeked out at her in her mind. The priest told her the story of how the boy had gotten those scars.

When the boy was small he had been carrying fuel to one of the food vendors. The can they gave him for the fuel was really too big for him to handle and it had no lid. He was walking up a steep hill to the food vendor but his left side had been soaked from all the fuel. He walked by a Korean man and for some cruel unknown reason the man threw a lit cigarette at the boy. He and the fuel immediately caught on fire. All the other Koreans around him just stood there watching. They did not want to get involved because they did not want to be held accountable. A black American soldier saw the whole horrid scene, put the fire out, and stayed with the boy until an ambulance came. The boy was in the hospital for a very long time and scars formed down the left side of his body. The soldier who had saved him came and sat with the boy every day for hours until the boy was released and then he quietly faded out of the boy's life.

Chapter Eight

The boy was a *chewing gum* boy. He would take packs of gum he bought for next to nothing and go in the bars and sell sticks of gum at a high price to the soldiers. He had also inherited a shoe shine kit from his older brother. That was how he made a living. The priest said that when it was cold out, the boys who sold gum all night would stay inside by coming and going to sell gum in all the different bars until they closed. Then they would take part of their earnings for the night and go to a 24-hour picture show to sleep in the warmth of the theater.

She was amazed that there were so many of these boys on the streets. She asked about orphanages. The priest frowned deeply and his shoulders went limp with sadness. What he told her next was like something out of horror stories. The children were housed together and there really was no room for all the children. Most orphanages were filled with Amer-Asian children, those who were half American and half Asian. There were extremely strict rules, small portions of food, while discipline was varied and extremely hard on the children. He gave her one example that had happened to the little boy.

He had broken a rule about food. He had been saving up small bits of food because he was planning an escape. When the adults found out they stripped him to his underwear, poured dried rice in a corner and made him kneel with his bare knees on the rice and they left him there until his knees bled. She could not imagine someone being so cruel to a child. The priest said most of the adults at the orphanages were terribly cruel and treated the children like they were prisoners of war. Every time a child could, they escaped and went back to living on the streets until the next round-up of street children began all over again. The priest had been protecting the boy from round-ups for about a year.

The priest then asked her something that would change the rest of her life. He was going to do missionary work near the border of North and South Korea. The boy would be on his own unless she would look after him. She readily agreed to have the boy come stay with her and her husband. Although the boy knew she was a friend of the priest, he was unsure of staying with the couple. The priest had taught her Korean words and phrases and she used those phrases and broken English to reassure the boy he would be safe with them. He agreed, but only came to their apartment after the clubs closed and just to sleep. He was so little he couldn't be more than nine. He fulfilled her maternal instinct. While he was there he taught her more words and phrases until her Korean was pretty good. He also taught her to never accept the first price a vendor gave her. Haggling made the vendor respect the person buying his goods and if she haggled with them long enough she would always get the best price.

As she became more fluent the boy began trusting her more and not only came home to sleep but also started hanging around with her. Then one night she had heard that the police had rounded up some boys off the street. She went to find the child she now considered her son, but had no luck in finding him. As she was walking up the hill away from the bars to get home to her apartment she felt like someone was following her. But when she stopped and turned back she could not see anyone there. She knew when danger was around from living on edge all the time in an alcoholic home. She knew that when she felt danger it was really there. Quietly she slipped into the courtyard and stood behind the gate waiting until she thought the person following her had gone on by the house. She silently slipped from behind the gate still feeling that she was in danger, so she scurried to the outside door to her apartment. She had to stop to bend over and take her shoes off. That's when the man came through the door. All she could do was squeak out her husband's name. Their apartment door flew open and her husband stood there with a four point razor edged throwing star in one hand and a knife in the other hand ready to be used at any second. The dirty smelly, horrible, Korean man immediately started apologizing in his native tongue. The whole time he was backing out door still vehemently apologizing.

She had been out searching for the boy and had searched until after dark. Her husband had been worried about her and was about to go looking for her right when the Korean man was going to attack her. He took his young wife inside and they got ready for bed together and although she was safe she had fitful dreams of where the boy might be. Because of the man trying to attack his wife, her husband started asking around the base if anyone knew of a safer place that was in his budget.

Finally they found a little three room apartment enclosed inside a building. There was a bathroom, a bedroom, and a place to have a kitchen. Stoves and refrigerators were luxury items in South Korea so they didn't have either one of those. But they did have a two burner electric stove that they cooked and warmed bath water on. They could have had hot water in this new apartment, but it cost more money and they just did not have it. They were in a safe place down the far side of the hill away from all the bars and vendors and that was what mattered most. The landlady allowed them to have friends over and to go to the roof and have barbecues and to picnic.

As it got hotter there were places to sunbathe, but the stench was so bad in the hotter weather she could not bear to go outside. She and her husband and their little Korean boy lived there as a family. They ate too much tuna casserole and a lot of vegetable beef soup until the American couple across the hall let them keep milk, butter, mayonnaise, and sandwich meat in their refrigerator just to be good neighbors. There was a wonderful couple downstairs that they had become friends with. The man was Japanese-American and was in the same unit as her husband. He had actually been the one to help them get the apartment. His wife was a tiny woman from the Philippines. She looked a lot like a Korean woman but with more rounded edges to her beautiful face. They had a big healthy baby boy, who looked even bigger next to his tiny, shorter than 4-foot tall mother. During the long, lonely days when the men were at the base the women would sit together and talk about their countries and customs and compare them to the Korean way of life. Her Korean son was always off meeting up with other *chewing gum* boys.

For her nineteenth birthday she, her husband, the little

43

boy, and a military liaison went to the Korean Consulate to see about adopting her beloved Korean child. She could tell by the heated discussion something was wrong and when the Army liaison came back to them she had bad news: the boy's papers said he was twelve. It seemed his older brother was adopted by another American couple and had used his younger brother's birth papers in order to get the adoption to go through. Then the hammer came down. Even if he did have his papers they would not be able to adopt the boy because she was only ten years older than the boy so she could not possibly be his mother. The last unbearable thing the liaison said was for the couple to go to an orphanage and pick out a new child because Amer-Asian children were easy to adopt.

A fierce motherly feeling sang in her heart: *but I took care of him all this time*. He had grown four inches and was healthy and always had a warm bed and plenty of food to eat. Now they were telling her she was not old enough to be his mother. She remembered the day of an orphan round up where they gathered all the children together and took them back to the orphanages. Her little boy had told the authorities he lived in a house with his mother and father so they came to the apartment with him in tow and asked if it was true. She had grabbed and hugged the boy and said, "Yes it is true, I am his mother!" But it was only true in her heart. She would never be given the right to take him back to America with her as her son.

The priest came back and they both begged the boy to go to the trade school where he would be fed and given a place to stay as he learned a trade. He was terrified of the orphanages. He thought the trade school would be similar and would not go. Her time in Korea was coming to an end. Soon she would fly out, leaving her Korean son to live back in the world of the *chewing gum* boys. That day came and the boy she considered her son went with her and her husband to the airport. The last thing he said to her was, "Goodbye Mother" in Korean and another shard of her was broken.

Chapter Nine

Her husband had to stay in Korea for a few more days to pack, do paperwork, clean, and return his gear. The other soldiers gave him a good-bye party and a plaque that simply stated they thought highly of him, that they knew he was a good soldier, and that he had worked hard for the unit.

Now she knew she was a grownup because she had flown over fourteen hours both to get to Korea and now to come home. She had taken care of a child who had grown and thrived under her care. She was sure everyone would see that she was all grown up.

She went home to her mother's house but was still treated the same. She felt childlike again and hated the fact that her mother could still affect her that way. Her husband went straight to his new duty station and was told he would only have to wait two months for housing. It was a perk of coming back from a single man's tour of duty. She was so happy she would be in her new home so quickly and that it would be on the Army Base in Fort Ord, California. She had to wait at her mother's house and what her mother decided she should do while waiting was to get a job. She was amazed that her mother was actually telling her, a married woman who had flown halfway across the world and back to get a job for two months. She was so shocked she got bold and told her she would not get a job! This was vacation time for her and she told her mother that even though her husband was already at the base and she had two months to wait she was not getting a job!

They were separated by distance but he was still the head of their household. He also thought it would be ridiculous for her to take a job for just two months. He told her mother he was capable of taking care of his wife, that she didn't need to work for two months, and the matter was settled. Her mother stood her ground on other matters and said even though she had been married almost two years, she would live by the rules while living under her roof.

There was one rule she broke every night. And that was a ridiculous curfew they had imposed upon her. She would get in the pick-up truck and head for her best friend's house. They would joy ride around the county and laugh and have fun till the wee hours of the morning. Then she would take her best friend home and return to her mother and father's house, slip into bed and be asleep before they woke up to start their day. She was not sure if her parents knew but she was a married woman, a real grownup, and she could do as she pleased! It was just her and her best friend, the night, and the wind.

But the two months passed and the friends knew soon they would part again. It was time for her to be a military wife once more with all the responsibilities that came with it. Her husband came home to get her and then they went to pick up the things they had in storage. Soon they were off again as a couple and it made her feel like the grownup she was becoming. Maybe she would get pregnant soon and she would get to use all the maternal instincts that she knew she had inside her and finally have her Knight's baby. It just had to be in California that she would get pregnant.

But she was too busy at first to even realize that dream hadn't come to pass. The housing situation on base was terrible. They were re-modeling half the housing and in order to relieve the housing problem, they had to rent out apartments off the base in secure neighborhoods. It was finally their chance to get an apartment. Their new apartment complex had fences and gates that had an electronic device to open, enter, or exit the apartment complex. She indeed felt grown up and even a little well off. Not only did they have security outside the apartment, there was an alarm system inside that needed a code into a key pad to make the apartment even safer than just having the gated community. What was so much more wonderful about the apartment was that at night time they would lay silent and still in the bed with their balcony doors open and they could hear the waves as they crashed against the seashore. The sound would be so peaceful it would ease them off to sleep. Because of fences, automatic gates, and large wooden walls around their balconies they felt safe enough to leave the door to their patio open just to hear the ocean sounds. They could hear the waves even though they were a mile from the beach.

All the time they were there, they had soldiers and their wives come over to play cards, to watch movies, and to just hang out with. The other soldiers and their wives and children seemed like a big family because they were all far from their homes, their loved ones, and friends they had grown up with. So they all bonded together and made a *military family*. There were plenty of children so her maternal instinct was fulfilled.

Her husband soon settled into the daily routine of working in the motor pool on the base where he served as a mechanic. His first sergeant, the man he was to report to first, was a Vietnam War Veteran who expected his soldiers to be top notch in their duties and their cleanliness. He seemed real unreachable at first, like he was mad at the world and it did not seem to her he ever let the world in. She would find out though that he had the kindest heart, told really funny stories, and loved to joke. When she threw all these traits together, she realized he was a really good first sergeant.

The first sergeant called her to come into his office one day and although she felt scared and a little ill at ease she went straight away to the appointment. He got to the point and plainly told her he knew she didn't work and he knew her husband was a really good soldier, so he figured she must have a good head on her shoulders. He leaned forward over the desk and talked as nicely as his gruff cigar smoking voice would let him and told her, "I need you to be head of "Family Support."

He said it in a way she knew she had better say yes, but she could feel herself become childlike because of the very fact she didn't know what "Family Support" meant. He saw it in her eyes that she did not know what that would entail, so he gave her the basic run down. She would meet each new military family when they had been processed into the unit and use the Family Support fund to buy them a welcome gift. She would visit with them and tell them all about the base, like where the commissary was located so they would be able to buy their groceries at a discounted price, where the Post Exchange could be found so they could shop the stores that had discounts on home goods, and all the other things the base had to offer them.

He went on to explain that her major duty would come if the base were ever to be put on Lock-Down. This meant that she would have to call each family and make sure the dependents had what they needed. Lock-Down meant that the post would be closed to all non-duty personnel, including all of the military dependents. There would be no calls allowed in or out of the base. He explained they would only know a Lock-Down had happened because the phones into the base would only have a busy signal and a person wouldn't be able to get a hold of their soldier, man or wife. That even meant past the regular time they were supposed to come home from the base. This was when the head of Family Support would need do her best to contact every wife or husband in the unit to let them know what was happening and to answer all questions that came up. It sounded as if it would be to simply tell each spouse that they were on Lock-Down and when she knew more she would tell them.

A few months later it happened. It worked just like the first sergeant said it would until the local news came on that night and told its viewers the base was on Lock-Down. Rumors were flying around that they would be deploying to South America to aid the Marines in a rescue mission. The calls suddenly came flooding in. Everyone wanted to know if it was true that their soldiers were going to South America. All she could say to them was remember it was a rumor and not a fact.

She had women calling for all kinds of problems. The

50

major ones she couldn't take care of, like how to get the family car off base. Another was from a lady who did not know anything about the base. She had never been taken there. She had no way to get her hands on any money unless her husband was home because he did not allow her to be on his bank account. The saddest by far was when a sixteen year old newly-wed bride had a friend call because she could not read or write and didn't know what to do. Those were the three major problems she had little clue as how to fix for the women, but she promised she would let them know immediately if she was told the soldiers were leaving to go to South America. She also informed them that if the soldiers were deployed, the base would be reopened after they left. A crew would be left behind to help them in every way they could, like if they had to go to the Army Emergency Relief to help get food and money. Also, they could get rides to the post to get their cars back. That seemed to satisfy the women who had those problems. It lasted three days, with women calling, crying, and asking if the soldiers had already been deployed or if they were still on the base. What was worse, they would beg her to tell them if she knew anything else, like they felt since she was head of Family Support she should know more. All she could tell them was to watch the news because they had more information than she did.

On the third day they went to stand down and she never heard another word from most of the women again. After it was all over and having to be strong for all of the women in the unit she laid down in their bed, curled up in a ball and let herself feel like a child. The dirty little girl with scars all over her came peeping out in her mind. The child was still halfway hidden by an object that was so blurry she couldn't make out what it was. She hated the little girl's image and she stuffed the vision way back in her brain so she did not have to see her or think about her again At that point, her regular headaches turned into migraines. She went to sleep until kisses on her forehead jolted her awake. It was him -- her Knight in shining armor that she loved so very much. He said the first sergeant was really proud of her and wanted to know about the problems that could not be taken care of in a timely fashion. They went to meet with him and she told him the three major problems she had faced. He said he would get with those soldiers and their families and square them away so they would be ready the next time a Lock-down came about. She left out all the other calls she had fielded while they were on Lock-Down. He smiled and his face cracked into a grin so big that it seemed like his old wrinkled face would completely crack into pieces as he said to her, "So you're not going to tell me about all the crazy calls you got day and night?" He looked at her intently and said, "I knew I could count on her." That was the end of the meeting and she was dismissed.

It was surreal like it had never happened, but she sure hoped another Lock-Down would not happen again while she was head of Family Support. She was very lucky because there was not another Lock-Down while they were stationed at Ft. Ord. She also knew to run the other way if another first sergeant ever asked her if she knew anything about Family Support. She did continue her Welcoming Rounds and helped every dependent that called to ask for information and steered them in the direction they. needed to go. She took her job very seriously and not until they came up with orders to go to Germany did she step down as head of Family Support.

She did not know it at the time but the first sergeant went through a lot of paperwork and a lot of channels to get her an award. This woman he had chosen as head of Family Support had truly been there for every dependent when she was needed. She was not just given any award -- she was given the highly esteemed *Molly Pitcher Award.* She stood in front of the unit formation when she heard the words inducting her into the small society of women that also held this prestigious award. And she felt proud of all she had accomplished.

The six month notice came and it said they would be going to Friedberg, Germany. She had wanted to go to Germany ever since she had read the book and seen the Shirley Temple movie called "Heidi." It was a childhood dream that was going to come true in six months. Since she had stepped down as head of Family Support, she had more time. She now had so much to do to prepare for the move. She hadn't had a period in years, which the Army doctors called amenorrhea, so when she started to bleed she just thought it was going to come now when she had so much to do. But this was different than a regular period. There was a lot of pain and the blood was thick, with thick pieces of congealed blood. It terrified her: maybe something happened and all those years of having amenorrhea had hurt something inside her. She made an appointment to get in as fast as she could but had to wait a week and all the while she had nightmarish thoughts of what it could be. Was it cancer? Was it a tumor? Was she free bleeding?

Her doctor's appointment came. He took some blood tests, did an exam, and told her the most despairing news he could have told her. She had been pregnant. The pregnancy had failed to make it through the first trimester. She didn't cry in front of the doctor who so crassly told her she had a baby inside her and it died. She went to her husband's unit, found him at the motor pool, and threw herself on him as she told him what all the bleeding meant. He tried everything to console her and nothing worked until he told her that it meant she could get pregnant. It stopped her in her tracks. The Army doctors just told her she had gone through menopause early when her periods had stopped suddenly when she was eighteen years old. But they were wrong. She had been a mother for almost three months and didn't even know about it. She could get pregnant! All those years thinking pregnancy was impossible, that it just would not happen for her. The fact was, the Army doctors did not know what they were talking about. She had lost her second baby but she was also astounded by what it meant: getting pregnant was a possibility.

The bleeding trailed off into a few small spots but didn't stop completely and about two and a half months later after she had just taken a seasonal position at a plus-sized clothing store for women since they would be going to Germany soon and might need the extra income. When pain gripped her again and since she had never totally quit bleeding from the miscarriage she called the woman's clinic on the base and they fit her right in. So there she was again, thinking horrid thoughts that something bad had happened because of the miscarriage and certainly now she would never have the chance to have a baby. She sat in the cold examination room with only a sheet to cover herself. They came and did blood work and after an examination the crass old doctor told her to get dressed and come into his office. She knew it was bad. He was going to take away the hope she had about being able to conceive. But what he told her hurt her more than that. He just said with no emotion that she had been pregnant again and that the pregnancy had once again terminated in the latter part of the first trimester. She could get pregnant but for some reason she could not keep the pregnancy longer than the first trimester. She asked him if he would help her get pregnant so she would know and maybe take it easy and get through that first trimester. He looked her in the eyes and said to her that she was too fat to get pregnant and if she did, she would die.

It stunned her. Not only did he have no feelings about the fact that she had just gone through her third miscarriage, he had insulted her about being overweight. She left the clinic feeling like her world was crushed. She had lost another baby and the doctor, a full bird colonel, had told her he would not help her get pregnant because she was so fat she would die. She was overweight. That part of it was true. But there were other women who were much bigger than her that had pregnancies and they did not have any complications. She was only one hundred and eighty two pounds and he had told her she was so fat that if he helped her get pregnant, she would die.

He said she would die. She was devastated. She was at home when her husband came in and she told him the heartbreaking news but when she told him what that colonel had said to her, he was outraged! The next morning he went to the first sergeant and the complaint went all the way up to the highest department: The Office of the Judge Adjutant General. A letter came back saying that the colonel denied he had ever said such a thing. It was her word against his. She found out later that these two men -- the man who had told her that awful thing and the man that was to review her case -- golfed together and she never had a chance at justice.

A good friend of another soldier in the unit told them how they could go off base and be seen by a civilian doctor. Their time was running out and it was almost time to go to Germany but her husband told her to go see if the civilian doctor could tell her anything. The friend told her the name of a civilian doctor and so she drove the twenty minutes and came face to face with a nun. The nun had to have special permission to become a doctor and all her earnings went to the church. She was only allowed to work in areas where the economy was depressed and she mainly worked with migrants that had no insurance. This was it! A doctor who became a doctor to truly help people! She looked at the records from the base, took some blood tests, and then showed her where the problem had been hiding. She had hypothyroidism. Her body needed medication to regulate hormones. The sweet precious nun had finally found out that all the missed periods and the three miscarriages had been caused by a disease that could be treated with medication. She put her on the lowest dose of medication for the condition and said when she got to her next duty-station they should recheck her hormones and then move her dosage up accordingly until it was balanced.

She would feel better physically and mentally. She left the nun doctor having hope!

.

Chapter Ten

The last month before her husband was sent ahead of her, they went back to her hometown to see her family. It was a short non-conflicting, actually loving visit and then he brought her to his Dad's house in a little town in Georgia. She was to wait there until she got her passport and visa in the mail and her flying orders and tickets. It took about twenty days for him to set up a household and all the paper work to be done. Two days before she was to leave, she started bleeding. That's when she saw the little girl with the blond hair again, sitting on the edge of a bed with sweat on her forehead, holding out her blood stained hands out looking as if to say, *what did it mean?* She shook her head hard -- why was her mind envisioning dirty dishwater? She could even smell marijuana and taste beer in her mouth. She knew not to make a big fuss about the vision or the bleeding because everyone would want her to stay in Georgia.

She bought all the necessities and when it was time for her to get on the bus to go to the airport, she was still bleeding. It was heavier than when she had the miscarriages and it seemed like it was flooding her. She got on the bus and finally at about eleven-thirty p.m. she made it to the airport bus station. It was closed. She told the driver she had a ticket that took her all the way to the airport and he told her this was the bus depot to change over, but no one was around. She asked when a bus would come and he said told her to check the schedule on the door. He took her bags off the bus and left her standing at the closed bus terminal all alone at night. The dirty blond haired little girl with the scars all over her peeked out in her mind. She saw the girl and mentally thought, *I feel as little and as scared as you but I have to be grown up and figure out what to do.*

She didn't know where she was in Atlanta but recognized that she was at a closed bus station and the next bus wouldn't run until after her flight took off in the morning. The only thing she knew to try was call a taxi cab. Thankfully the bus station had a payphone. She looked up the number in the tattered phone book and called a taxi company. She explained where she was and where she needed to be. They told her they would be there in about ten minutes. Good to their word, they were there within ten minutes. She got in the taxi cab, thankful she had extra money with her and the driver headed off into the night. All of the sudden she felt scared that anything could happen, that he could take her anywhere because she was just a small town girl in this huge city that was a maze of roads and lights.

Finally she saw it! It was the Atlanta Georgia International Airport looming ahead on the lighted strip of road. He took her right to the area she needed to be in. She paid him the fare and gave him a five dollar tip. She didn't know the normal tip for a taxi cab driver because she had never been anywhere that she needed to take a trip in one. He seemed happy and helped her with her luggage. It was around one in the morning. She walked into the airport to find it ghostly quiet. She thought to herself, *where had the people gone?* There was no one around to even ask that question. Her mind started thinking quickly: did they not have flights all night long? She was alone. She found her gate and sat down to wait the three hours until her flight from Atlanta to JFK airport would depart. She went to the bathroom and found out she had bled through to her pants but she had her suitcases with her still and changed into a clean outfit. She knew she was bleeding badly and that she might need to call an ambulance, but all she could think was that she just needed to get to Germany. She cleaned herself up and was worried about bleeding through again so she took some things out of the bag she was going to carry on the plane, placed them in the suitcases, and put two clean outfits into the bag she would take with her on the plane in case she might have that problem again. She also bought more sanitary napkins in case she kept bleeding that badly. She left the bathroom and was ready to wait for her flight. She realized she was totally alone. A man with gold chains around his neck and rings on all of his fingers came up to her and started saying things like he could really make some money off of her. She was from a small town but she knew what he was and what he was referring to. She became a frightened child again. The next thing he said would change her life's reality. He told her she had some big old boobs and they could make a lot of money with them.

She could not hear anything else he was saying because she was in a poorly-lit room with dust clouding out the sunlight that was streaming in from the east. And there upon a bed lay the older friend of her sisters. The girl was in her late teens. She was naked on the bed. She had huge breasts, the size of the watermelons her father brought home in summer. She was almost a big girl because she had just turned five but something didn't seem right. She had come to that house to get her sisters to come home because their mother wanted them. The girl on the bed told her, "We are playing house." She could be the baby, while the girl on the bed would be the mommy. She didn't know why she felt funny in her tummy but she felt like she was going to run. The girl on the bed said words that made her want to be a part of playing house. She told her to come real close and her brave five year old self went near the bed. The girl on the bed told her she was going to let her be the baby and she going to feed her. They were actually going to let her play! They never had before and she was happy that she was going to be the baby until the girl on the bed told her to suck her boobs and to act like she was drinking milk. She felt like something was wrong but she wanted to be included in playing house so badly that she did what she was told. Immediately the girl on the bed started making funny breathing noises and it scared her so much she ran away back across the street to her own house. She felt like she had done something bad but she really did not know what. She knew she did not want to play house with her sisters' friends anymore.

It was just a flash in her mind. It seemed to take a long time to remember that day but she became aware it had only taken seconds for the memory to come back and to end. Now back to reality, she had the funny sick feeling in her stomach and the scary man was taunting her. He kept saying how he wanted her to come with him and she would make him a lot of money. She had just remembered something horrible that had happened to her as a child in an empty airport with no one around but her and the pimp. She was beyond thinking clearly and repeated over and over, "That did not happen, it did not happen!" And the dirty scarred up little blond haired child came peeking out in her mind. She could see the girl's scars and how dirty and frightened she was but she crouched behind something and she couldn't make any sense out of it. She realized that was not the most pressing thing to worry about. The pimp was watching her and he must have realized she wasn't thinking straight because he came towards her and all she could say was, "God help me." She heard the words come out of her mouth but did not know if it was because the memory had come back or because the man was getting closer. Out of the corner of her eye she saw another man coming. She was terrified that there would be two against her. She was not going to get to go to Germany after all. But all of the sudden the man moved from the shadows and she saw he was an Army soldier.

She started thinking quickly and if the soldier caught on and helped her out she would be safe. As the soldier came closer she pointed at him when the pimp turned to look and she said in a loud voice, "I'm with him and he won't like you talking to me like that!" The soldier suddenly became aware of what was happening and told the pimp in a menacing voice that he better watch what he was saying to her. The pimp told the soldier that he had said nothing wrong, that he just wanted her to be safe and he knew a place he could take her. The soldier continued playing the part and told the pimp, "She's with me so she is safe enough. She doesn't need your help." The pimp slowly turned, walked down the empty corridor, and was out of view within a few minutes.

Tears were rolling down her cheeks and the soldier asked in a kind voice if she was all right. He would never know that her tears were because of what had happened to her when she was five so she just told him that she had just been shocked. In truth, she had just been shocked by a memory that had long stayed hidden in her mind. With all her might, she pushed the thoughts back down in the depths of her memories. He introduced himself and she did likewise. They found out they were both going to Frankfurt, Germany. She thought, "Thank you God, for putting this soldier in my life right when I needed help!"

They talked until the stewardesses arrived. At that point, everybody started showing up and boarded the plane. It took off with both of them aboard headed for JFK. She got off the plane at the JFK airport and had to go outside and across a street to get to the International flights. She looked up and it was like she was in the middle of the city -- big skyscrapers filled the sky. She knew though if she did not want to miss the flight she would have to quit looking at the buildings and go to the International Flights side. Once there she had to go to the bathroom and check to see if she had bled through. She had and as she cleaned herself up, she was thankful she had the opportunity and common sense to put the extra clothes in the bag she carried with her on the plane before she had checked her luggage in at Atlanta. While changing she noticed she was still bleeding very heavily. All she wanted to do was get to Germany and she was on the last leg of the trip. She could do it! She could make it!

She waited for her plane to board and once on board

found her seat was on the aisle. She could get out easily and there right beside her was that soldier. It brought back all the memories that she had become aware of and immediately the dirty scarred blond headed girl appeared in her mind but she just shook her away. Here he was, her Atlanta hero, sitting right next to her. She found the bathroom, checked and cleaned herself up, and felt better now that she was on the flight to Germany and this would be the last part of her journey. She was very worried she would bleed through so she went to the bathroom often and checked herself. She was feeling very weak and tired and finally went to sleep and hours later landed in Frankfurt, Germany. She saw her husband right away. She was very weak and could barely carry the bag that she had brought on the plane. But she had actually made it to Frankfurt, Germany! A lifelong childhood dream had come true and there was her Knight with a giant stuffed animal and flowers.

He took one look at her and knew she was sick. She told him about the bleeding and he said there was a small medical unit on the base that she had flown into so they headed straight for the car. He half-carried her to the car and then drove her to the medical unit but they said they were not equipped to handle a major problem. The soldier at the medical unit told him it would take about an hour to get to the U.S military hospital in downtown Frankfurt. They got back into the car and he was going to turn towards the hospital but she said, "Just take me home."

And that's where they went. First onto the Autobahn, then on city streets, all the way down into small streets of a village. He took her inside, helped her get clean and put her pajamas on, and she drifted back off to sleep. It was afternoon when she went to sleep but when she woke up the full sunlight of midday was upon her.

Chapter Eleven

How long had she slept? She immediately went to check about the bleeding. But there were only tiny spots. She was amazed after all the bleeding she had been having there were only spots. She was still weak and unfamiliar with the apartment. She did not remember anything except riding for a long time in the car. She stood to her feet, caught her balance, and remained very still until the room stopped spinning. She was obviously in the bedroom. It had a bed in the room but nothing on the walls and no other furniture and no closet. The bear from the airport that said, "I love you" in German lay close by the bed. She walked into the living room and there were silver boxes connected to regular things like the stereo and the television. She found out later the silver boxes were transformers There was no furniture in the living room except for two tattered chairs placed in front of the television set. She already knew that the bathroom was in the hall and she turned left into a very small kitchen. It had a table and two chairs that filled up the room so that she had to maneuver her way around by the sink to get to the refrigerator. She opened it but it was bare. She found a note on the table from her husband saying he was at the base in Friedberg where he was stationed, but would come home by lunch with groceries. It wasn't too long after she found the note that he did come home.

He had freshly baked bread from a bakery, fresh cheese and meats from a deli, and some American food as well. She immediately opened a cola and sat down in the kitchen chair. She was still weak and dizzy from all the standing, but she knew she would get better now that the bleeding had almost completely stopped. Her husband suggested the fresh bread, cheese and meats to start with. She was famished. With all the worrying about the bleeding she did not know when or where she had her last meal. He showed her how to put the creamy fresh butter on the sides of the round breads, picked his favorite meat and cheese, and gave it to her to eat. She was so famished that all she knew was that all together it tasted great. He sliced two more pieces off the warm crusty bread, buttered them and let her choose what meat and cheese she would like to try. She just picked by how pretty they looked and found her combination quite delightful.

They sat, talked about many things, and ate the bread, meats, and cheese until they were all gone. The other things were put in the refrigerator because the kitchen had no cabinets. It seemed cabinets were a luxury item in this country. He told her he had to go back to the base in Friedberg for a little while but she could come because his commander had given him a couple of days off to show her around the base and community. Where they lived was considered economy housing because it was far away from the base and they had to pay rent to live there. It was just like renting a house anywhere, but her husband had found this quaint quiet village with an apartment they could afford and it was decent except for having nothing on the walls and having almost no furniture. He said as they were on the way back to the base that he would show her the house where a buddy of his

lived with his American-French wife.
They met their neighbors and she immediately liked
the couple. She was happy to find out they had two
small boys that were two and four. The boys were
playful and sweet and being around them fulfilled her
maternal instinct. They loved being held, rocked, and
cuddled, They loved anyone who would pay attention
to them. The women became friends instantly and
since the American-French woman could drive she
offered to teach her almost everything she would need
to survive as an American in a foreign country. But this
was her first trip to the base and it would be shared
only with her husband.
The scenery was so lit up with colors that were so
bright and vivid it seemed as if a giant had come
through with the brightest paints and colored
everything in the lines with colors that she had never
seen before. On the way he showed her a Hunter's
restaurant that had fresh wild game and told her they
would go there one day. But the most impressive
things she had seen were the sunflowers. Fields and
fields of sunflowers and their heads were turned
directly towards the sun.
They traveled on through the little town that
surrounded the Army base. They went to his barracks
then up to his room to collect his things when his
roommate, otherwise known as his *room dog,* came
in and introduced himself to her. He was a very happy-
go-lucky guy and they immediately took to each other.
He grabbed a sleeping bag, some clothes, some
tennis shoes, and came along for the weekend.
They left the barracks and her husband took her to the
unit headquarters to show her the day room that had
pool tables, ping pong tables, books and reading

chairs. It was where the soldiers could go and have fun during their leisure hours. Everyone else was busy and to tell the truth there was nothing remarkable about any of the advanced ranking soldiers and officers and because of that she never even got to know them. Next he took her to the motor pool and introduced her to a lot of hard-working happy fellow soldiers who were very kind to her. As a surprise, he took her to the barber shop and introduced her to the man that had cut Elvis Presley's hair the whole time he was stationed at Friedberg Army base. There were pictures of him cutting Elvis's hair and it was like walking back in time. They went off base to eat lunch at a very small kiosk and they stood in line for what her husband said was the best gyros and french fries she would ever eat!

She waited in the long line and was given this thick tortilla like bread with roasted meat and vegetables and a white sauce on it. They got the fries and lots of mayonnaise she thought was for the gyros but he poured the packages of mayonnaise out on the edges of the gyrod paper and dipped his French fries down in it like they dipped fries in ketchup in America. She was unsure of following suit but she did and was surprised that the French fries and the mayonnaise did not taste like anything she had eaten in America. It was very different and very, very good. Then the real taste test came because she was going to try her very first gyros and she had been promised it would be delicious. She took a bite and it was so good she ate it down quickly and licked the white sauce off her fingers. It was her first taste of lamb and she liked it very much!

The sun was starting to go down and with his *room*

dog in tow they all were on their way back to their little village. On the way she saw the sunflower's faces had turn toward the falling sunset. It was amazing that every face had followed the sun all day long in some Godly symphony and now they would bow their heads until the sunshine would bring their happy faces back around into the morning light.

The whole day was a wonderful adventure. Her husband taught her the German names for bakery, deli, and the grocery store. He took her to the bus depot and showed her how to get to the base if she could not get him on the phone.

They went back to the American-French girl's house and she was so friendly and kind to her all over again. They hit it off so well she told her to come to her house any day, even every day because most of the time she would have the family car and get them to and from Friedberg for more adventures. Her new American-French friend knew the area very well and would take her on outings to the park to feed the black swans. The boys loved to go feed the swans and they would rent a paddle boat and take a trip around the lake. It was the best part of the week for all of them when they went and it was always a major adventure.

Weeks turned into months when the American-French girl decided to get a job on the base. Since she was the only neighbor that knew the boys and was right by the house, she was asked if she would come babysit. She agreed wholeheartedly and everything changed. Everybody had a job and everyone seemed happy. She slowly got better and thought everything was going to be easy from there on in.

Right around a month after she started taking care of the boys, she started bleeding again. She was sure it would stop, but it wasn't like the first time: it didn't stop in three days. It just kept coming and coming and she would go to babysit the kids and have to rest most of the day, doing the bare essentials for the children.

A day came and she could feel the beating of her heart as it pounded against her chest. She called her husband at the motor pool. She told him about her heart and how she couldn't breathe and the American-French lady had already left for work. She asked if he could come take her to the post medical unit. She thought she was having a heart attack! Her Knight was there within minutes. He also had father of the boys with him and she felt better when she knew they would be safe, too.

He got her to the car and to the medical unit, where they immediately started working on her. They had quickly ruled out that she was having a heart attack. But something was wrong and a blood test revealed she did not have enough blood in her body. They called for a German ambulance to come take her to the U.S. military hospital in Frankfurt all the while giving her an I.V. of fluids to rehydrate her. Her Knight was at the hospital when they arrived but was immediately pushed out of the way. The nurses and the doctor were frantically moving around her and the next thing she knew, she was in a hospital bed. She still felt weak and tired but then the doctor came in and explained they had stopped the bleeding with birth control pills. He told her she had lost a lot of blood, so much that she really needed a transfusion. He explained quite calmly that even though she needed a blood transfusion that the blood they had in Germany was not like blood in America. At that time they did not screen it for AIDS. She would be taking a big risk if she took the blood transfusion. He said with complete bed rest, heavy doses of iron, and proper nutrition she would slowly get better. Not wanting to play roulette with her life she did just that. She went home to get some bed rest.

She slept many days. Her Knight woke her, sat her up, fed her, and was loving toward her. One day she sat up by herself. Her head spun around so she lay back down, but she was awake and her heart wasn't pounding against her chest anymore. By the time her Knight came home that evening she was able to sit up by herself. He fed her foods that were high in nutrition and gave her the iron to take. Her first day awake and alert, She was disoriented and did not know what day it was at the time. Her husband told her he brought her home from the hospital two days after they admitted her. She had slept on and off for days. He only woke her up to feed her and give her the iron that he had received from the doctor when they left the hospital. He told her in the mornings he gave her the mega doses of iron and foods high in nutrition but she was barely able to sit and eat, and that she slept the rest of each day. This had gone on for nine days. The tenth day was when she sat up.

It was near Thanksgiving and her American-French friend invited the couple to come eat with them since she was still weak. The American-French girl prepared a wonderful mixture of American, German and French foods for Thanksgiving dinner. It was the biggest Thanksgiving feast she had ever seen. She tried all the food except escargot: she just could not make herself eat snails.

Chapter Twelve

She grew stronger every day, which was good news because the post housing authority had found housing for them off base. The housing on base was full so just like they did at Fort Ord, California, the Army rented off post housing to put families into so they could meet the housing needs of the soldiers. The place they were given was built into the side of a hill. There was a window in the kitchen where she could look up and see people walking around, but when she walked outside the back the house was floor level to the ground. She loved that and the fact none of the rooms were square. There was a big living room and dining room together but they seemed like they were completely separate because of how much room there was between them. There were only two bedrooms and neither of them was square either.

They moved in and had a house warming party. They invited all her husband's buddies from the motor pool and her American-French friend's family. There were flowers, cakes, and a lot of German beer. The soldiers loved their German beer. They made homemade pizzas that were two inches thick with all kinds of toppings. Even her husband's *room dog* was there. There were also two brothers there that were stationed very close to each other. The next door neighbor came downstairs and introduced himself and his daughter, a curly brown-haired, blue-eyed child that stole her heart immediately.

They were all gathered down in their house. It was a

fun night and when everyone first arrived she told them to give her their car keys because no one was going to drink and drive. The only people that left were the American-French friend and her family because her friend was the designated driver and had had nothing to drink. Everyone was spread out all over the house on the carpet and were fast asleep. She thought it might be very uncomfortable but these were soldiers who slept anywhere they could during field maneuvers. A nice thick carpet and a blanket and pillow made everyone happy.

Every night they would come home with her husband bring food and beer, hand over their keys, and get up early enough to get back to their units and do their morning ritual of getting ready for the day. Suddenly she realized she had inherited a family. Soon they were calling her and her husband Mom and Pop. They were a motley crew but they fulfilled her maternal instinct.

For about a year this strange family lived sweetly together. Playing cards, or playing video games and drinking German beer was the main entertainment But somewhere deep inside her she knew something was coming: the little girl with the blond hair and scars on her body peeked out more and more with a terrified look on her face. Oh yes, she knew something was coming and the feeling went all the way to her soul.

There were rumors that the soldiers were to be sent to the Persian Gulf at the time when the Desert Storm/Gulf War would just be starting. They all held their breath when the first rumor said they would be gone by Thanksgiving, but she ended up making a wonderful Thanksgiving feast for them. Everyone was tense and on edge, so there was even more German beer. They were then told they wouldn't have Christmas with their families. But that came and passed too. The gift giving was very loving -- all the guys chipped in and bought her a Black Forest Cuckoo clock that meant the world to her. But all the rumors were over when they set the date for the beginning of January and the day actually arrived. Early in the morning they had their gear and loaded up on buses that would take them to the planes that would fly them far away into an unknown war. The dependents were all left behind. Some were crying, some were angry, but most of them were stunned. Two thoughts would not leave her mind: if anything happened to her Knight she would never bear his child and something was coming. It was still coming. And another shard broke off.

Chapter Thirteen

The small off base housing community had only women dependents left. All of the women forgot petty squabbles and started working with each other. Being from Florida, she loved to shovel snow it wasn't even like a chore to her She was like a kid with a special treat. She shoveled everyone's sidewalks and steps to their houses and put down the chemical substance that was to prevent the paths from freezing again. It also made a layer between the slippery sidewalks and their shoes. All the women were grateful and she felt happy that she could do this one thing to help all of them in this tense time of war.

One day suddenly all contact from all the soldiers was cut off and she did not hear anything from her Knight. She had waited to hear from him for a month and there was no word. No word from any of the men. She couldn't take the not knowing and so she went to the post, wrote a check, and bought a ticket to go back home.

She knew to take her air sickness medicine and she was on her way to America. The trip to the airport was the scariest thing she thought she had embarked upon until she sat in her seat at the airport and they announced a small delay to de-ice the wings of the plane! The snow was heavy and she thought maybe this was a bad idea but it was too late to think of things like that because she was watching the runway fall beneath them as they climbed through the snow laden clouds and flew above the tumult that was the snow storm beneath them. The flight seemed very long and filled with fearful thoughts of why her Knight could not contact her anymore.

Her flight landed in Orlando, Florida, but she needed to get to Tampa, Florida. So she had to find the gate to board the final flight of her trip. Everyone she asked told her that it was on the ground level, so she thought of having to board the plane from a tall staircase just like in the movies. When she got to her gate they asked her how much she weighed. That frightened her so she told them twenty pounds heavier than the two-hundred and twenty three pounds she was and they looked her up and down and asked her to get on the baggage weighing apparatus. For some unknown reason they needed to know her exact weight. This had never happened to her in all of her flying adventures before and she was baffled. Then they told her to go through the glass doors and the stewardess would seat her. When she walked out onto the tarmac there was this tiny little plane with propellers and a stewardess waiting by three steps that would take her into the plane. She thought, *"This cannot be my flight."* She always got on big airplanes that flew all over the world. This was a tinker toy compared to those planes. She asked the stewardess at the door was this really her flight. The fake smiling stewardess assured her she was on the right plane and showed her to a seat that was on one side of the plane. Her side of the plane had one seat against the windows from the front to the back of the plane. There were rows with two seats on the other side of the plane with three men sitting alone on different seats. There was one man behind her and that is when it hit her. They had to know exact weights to fly the plane at a level height. That's when it dawned on her this was what they called a commuter flight, which were small planes that travelled short distances back and forth every day. Yes, she was on a small commuter flight bound for Tampa, Florida.

She tried to calm herself and thought opening the window shade and watching the plane leave the airstrip behind would make her feel better, so she opened her window shade and right outside her window was the propeller. Watching it made her sick so she shut the shade. She heard the whirring of the propeller as the plane started down the runway and faster than the bigger flights she was up in the air. She was so frightened that for the whole commute, she listened intently to the sound the propeller made.

She was so entranced by its normal humming sound that she did not realize when the plane began to descend, finally landed on the airstrip, and stopped safely on the tarmac. When she stepped out of that tinker toy plane, she felt like it was all surreal but she followed the others up to level one and back down to ground level to get her baggage.

She saw her eldest sister peek from behind a pole and she felt such relief. One by one her siblings and her mother and father were all there. It was like a family reunion! They had not sent just one family member to pick her up -- they all came! There was laughing and crying and hugging going on. And they got her bags and all got in their vehicles to make a convoy back to her hometown an hour away. She was overwhelmed. She felt like a shard would break off from not having heard from her Knight in over a month and flying on a tinker toy airplane. But then having a large family reunion when everything should have felt like it was finally coming together, she felt safe enough to let herself fall apart. There was no consoling her. Her family just tried to say things that would make her feel better.

By the time she arrived home, she felt calmer and safer. Her younger sister had an eleven month old daughter and was eight months pregnant. She decided to stay with her sister and try to help with the children. Her niece did not know anything about this new person that came to stay at her house and was very unsettled by that fact. If she got mad about anything she would hit her aunt like everything bad that happened was because of her. It did not hurt and it was so cute that it just made her laugh.

The first month there flew by and soon it was time for the new baby to be born. Her sister gave birth to a big, healthy, beautiful, baby boy after a long difficult labor. When her one year old niece finally got to see her Mama again, after three days, and meet her new baby brother, she seemed unimpressed. But, the new aunt, was happy to cuddle the baby while her sister grabbed up her sweet little brown haired, princess, kissing and playing with her.

They went back home from the hospital to her sister's two bedroom cottage in the country. Her sister was breastfeeding her new nephew and most of the time her niece could not get up in her mama's lap. It made her laugh to see her niece try to get in between the baby and her mama. But even those sweet precious moments could not erase the worry from her mind. It had been months since she had heard anything from her husband and she missed him so much.

A few weeks after the baby was born, late in the middle of the night, her sister came and woke her. She kept repeating, "He is on the phone, your husband is on the phone!" She woke up immediately and grabbed the phone -- was it him, was it really him? And then he spoke her name and when she heard his voice, it calmed all her fears. He was safe. He didn't know when he would return but he knew it would be very soon. She went back to bed after the call, feeling calm and at peace. As she was falling back to sleep she could feel the months of tension fade away into the first peaceful night's sleep she had since he had left.

Everything was going well until she got a call from her neighbor in Germany, who said the apartment above hers had a pipe burst. It had leaked down onto her ceiling, which had fallen down into her apartment. The Army needed to know exactly what damages had occurred so they could replace the items that were destroyed. She quickly booked a flight out of Orlando, Florida and headed back to Germany.

While in route to the airport she realized it was the day of their sixth wedding anniversary. She flew back to Germany and went to her apartment to detail the damage for the Army. Most of the damage was to her ceiling and the cushions to the couch on its wooden frame. All they needed was for a cleaning team to come dry clean them. But what no one could fix, and what the Army could not replace was her family album full of her wedding pictures. She salvaged what she could, keeping only the ones of her and her Knight together. The pictures of the flowers, a picture of the cake, and one of the wedding party others. brought back bad memories and even though some were still salvageable, she tossed those out, too. She rebuilt her new family album with those few pictures and the pictures of her Korean son. Now all she had to do was wait for the Gulf War to end and her husband would return soon.

They waited for news from the units their husbands were in and little by little, dates were set for the different units to come home. Then something that was started as a horrible rumor turned out to be true. One man had been killed and another severely injured in an explosion at the encampment site that her husband's unit was in. There were no names, just confirmations. There would be no contact until each soldier's family had been contacted and given the news in person. They all waited. They were all sick from not knowing and then the names were released. Although the women knew the soldiers names, they did not know them personally. Now the Army could move on to getting their soldiers back home. It meant her husband's unit would finally be coming home. They flew in to Frankfurt, Germany and came home on buses, but no one knew which bus their husband might be on. The women moved from bus to bus, calling for their husbands finally hearing that one voice that they were calling for and reuniting.

She started to panic -- her husband, her Knight was nowhere to be found. She called out his name and her voice rose above the crowd. She had found all of the motley crew that came and stayed at her house. They were all well and safe, but she could not find her Knight.

Suddenly there he stood.

She was stunned and started laughing, crying, and kissing that face that was so beautiful it went right down to his soul. Her Knight was home.

Soon the men that made up their *military family* were back with them at their home playing cards and solving video games. It was not the same anymore though. Their unit was in the middle of disbanding and they were all being sent back to the States and to their new permanent duty stations. Their little family was sent in all directions in the United States. They would be going to Fort Hood, Texas where it all began for them. Their next door neighbor would be sent there also and at least it seemed part of the family would stay intact.

Everything was set and they all said their goodbyes. Each day a few more soldiers and their families would be sent home. They had time to themselves and started talking about important things like how they knew they were meant to be together and that they really wanted to start their family. Her face was shining brightly as she talked about having a baby again. It was the first time she had spoken about getting pregnant to him again since the last of the three miscarriages.

They went back to the States and visited their families as they made their way back to Texas. In January of 1991 they were stationed back with some of their friends at Fort Hood, Texas. But the scarred, dirty, little girl with the frightened little face peeked out in her mind and she knew something bad was coming. Something very bad was yet to come.

Chapter Fourteen

She had dreamed about the little house they would find to live in and it was exactly like the one in the dream she had. There was a small kitchen and a great big bedroom, a dining area and a living room, a bathroom, and a second bedroom for when the baby came. She knew she wasn't pregnant but she just knew coming back here to Fort Hood had to be a sign she that would finally get pregnant. She knew she had to get in with the infertility doctor and get him to help her restart her periods. The first thing she knew they would do is put her back on thyroid medicine. She did that through her family physician and got back on track with it but it didn't help. Each month came and went and she did not get pregnant She started having bad dreams of people trying to hurt her but when she would awaken the people's faces and names were gone with nothing left of the dreams except the feeling something bad was coming.

By the next summer they got housing on the base and they settled into a routine of day to day life. Even though it was quite boring, she had made friends with some of the other families that came from the same base in Germany. When the guys were out on maneuvers she would sleep in, get her housework done, and would get together with some of her friends. The women would play cards all night. They all stuck together when their husbands were gone. The routine was always the same. Almost every day the guys would be gone the women would gather together at night.

One morning she began to bleed. It was like the other times when she had bled -- it kept flowing nonstop. She stayed at her house for three days because she had to change so frequently. When she started getting weak and knew it was not going to stop, she called the infertility doctor that was trying to help her to get pregnant. The doctor squeezed her in on an emergency basis and after she was checked her out, she was told she was bleeding too much, too fast. She would have to go into surgery for dilation and curettage, what the doctors commonly referred to as a D and C. She was given a time to come back in the early morning hours to get the minor surgery. She had never been put to sleep and was so afraid she would not wake up. But her Knight had been sent back from maneuvers and he was there. He said everything would be okay.

The next morning he took her to the hospital. She signed in, was sent to a room that she was assigned to, and found there was another female patient in the bed beside hers. They were both having surgery and so were both given directions of the same kind -- wash with Betadine from head to toe and make sure to scrub everything real hard. They were given new surgical gowns to put on after they washed and funny little fluffy booties. Then they were to make it back to their beds and get in as if they were going to sleep.

When they got back to their room their charts were on their beds. She was curious and picked hers up. She glanced over it and saw the word hysterectomy. Her mind screamed, "No!" They couldn't do that! She quickly called a nurse into the room. The nurse took her chart, looked at it, took the other woman's chart, and looked at it. She smiled like a small mistake had been made, and simply switched the charts around to put them back on the correct beds. They had almost given her a hysterectomy and the nurse just acted like it was a small mistake! Now she was even more frightened about what would happen to her while she was asleep and if she would ever wake up was all she kept thinking about.

The time for her surgery came, the right chart was on her bed, and everything seemed to be in place. The orderlies came and wheeled her bed down the corridor beyond the doors where her Knight had to wait and then they helped her slide onto the surgical table. They put the mask over her nose and mouth and told her to count backwards from one hundred but she only remembered getting to ninety-eight before she was waking up. Her Knight was there and she was pulling him to her saying, "I love you, I love you so much." But all she could hear was laughter as the petrified anesthesiologist removed himself from her all encompassing grasp. He was not her Knight and she realized she was still in the operating room.

Once she was back in her room the doctor came by and said the D and C had been very successful. The doctor went on to say that she would never have been able to bleed the lining out that had built up inside her body. It had been building up layer by layer until it had formed a mass. It was a good thing they found it and the surgery would help her get back on the right track to getting pregnant. She was told to go home, stay off her feet a few days, and everything would be back to normal. She was put on high doses of iron again.

However, she could not rest and relax -- she had come close to having her dreams of having a baby stolen from her by the simple act of putting a chart on the wrong bed. The surgery may have been simple but going through it left her unsteady. She slept during the day. At night time she was wide awake, staring at the little blond haired girl with blood on her hands. She envisioned some dirty gray dish water, smelled marijuana, and tasted beer in her mouth but she still did not know what it meant. She was not pregnant and had little hope of getting pregnant. The only two children she could count on seeing were the two in her mind and she didn't understand what either of them meant or why they were there.

Her husband went back out for a two week field maneuver and she was left all alone. She could not get pregnant and a horrible sadness permeated her mind, body and soul. There was no one she could talk to and tell them she was seeing things in her mind and that it was even affecting her sense of taste and smell. All she could think about that maybe the sexual abuse she went through had done some kind of damage that kept her from being able to get pregnant. Or that the abuse was somehow responsible for making her lose the baby before the first trimester was over.

She felt like her thoughts were boiling with all these pictures of dead babies, the moaning man's son, the rape, and other terrifying visions she didn't know that belonged to her, like a child being hurt over and over. She began to wonder if that the little girl being hurt over and over was really her. Was she the scarred dirty little girl and was she the blond haired child with sweat on her forehead and blood in her uplifted hands seeing dirty dishwater, smelling marijuana, tasting beer in her mouth? She still did not know what it all meant. The thoughts were racing through her head:

86

pictures, pain, noises, smells, trees and pigs! She wanted it to stop. She wanted to have peace but there was no peace. There was a dark fog that surrounded her and stole her mind away until there was only one thought left in her mind. She could make it stop. She could make it stop forever. She knew how. She would just go to sleep. But her heart knew her future would be gone forever. That her Knight would find her like that and it would scar his beautiful soul, so she dialed the number for information and told them she needed the number to a rape crisis line. Because that was it right? She had been raped and that was what was causing all this hellish pain.

She had just kept it inside all these years, only telling her mother, who not only did not believe her but had insisted that her rapist's mother make her wedding dress. She dialed the number, a woman's voice came on the line, and she told her she had been raped at sixteen and all the thoughts in her head made her want to go to sleep and never wake up. The woman talked sternly but lovingly and soon had her calmed down. The woman said there was help in the world. The Army had a place she could go and see a doctor who would help her with the crazy thoughts she was having. Then the lady said, "Please have hope." The lady also gave her the number to the doctor on the Army base. *"Please have hope, please have hope"* echoed through her mind. She stayed up all night long and when she knew the doctor was in she called and talked to his secretary. She told the secretary about the conversation she'd had with the nice lady on the Rape Crisis line. The secretary said there had been a cancellation at one o'clock and to be early to do some paperwork.

She took a shower, dressed, sat in the living room in some kind of trance, and waited until it was time to leave. The doctor's office was not very far away and she went early like the woman had asked her to do. She was trying to fill out the paperwork but it was hurting her head. She realized suddenly she didn't even know what year it was anymore! She only filled out the parts where she could actually remember the answers. When she took it back to the secretary, she asked in a small childlike voice, "What year is it?"

The woman looked stunned and asked, "Do you mean what the date is today?"

Her mind had been jumbled for so long she didn't know what year it was. She handed the paperwork to the secretary and left the woman standing there with a stunned look on her face and went back to sit down. It was building inside her, the feelings, the emotions, the devastation, and the terror of it all. She just sat there and it built in her until her head throbbed.

An Army doctor in his work uniform introduced himself to her and said, "Come to my office." She followed him and a man followed her. He introduced the man and said something about school and research and asked if could he stay. She said yes and he asked her what was happening. It all came out of her like she was vomiting -- just word after word, horror after horror. Finally when nothing else came out, she sat there and waited for him to tell her the things she could do to feel better. He pushed back his chair and he said he was sorry but he could not help her. He handed her a piece of paper. "I am referring you to off base counseling." He said. "Here is a list of providers that you can see."

"*No!*" Her mind screamed. "*No!*" Her thoughts were lit

with fury because she had told him everything! *Everything!* How could he just let her tell her whole story to him and some research student and then calmly say he could not help her? Rage built in her. She felt like she had turned into a mad dog and she wanted to tear him to pieces. She had told him the secrets, all of them. She told him everything they had done to her and all he could do was give her a piece of paper with names on it?

Just as she was going to attack him, the numbness came. From the back of her neck all the way over her head into her arms and legs she became totally numb. She couldn't think thoughts other than basic commands. Stand, walk, follow, go outside, get in truck. She sat there, feeling numb for how long, she never knew. She was afraid to go home because there was a gun in that house, but she had to go there because it was the only place she could go.

She called the Rape Crisis line and was hysterical. Finally the counselor calmed her down. She told the counselor, *"He gave her a piece of paper with names on it."* How was she supposed to know who to go to and trust with her story? How could she go to one of those people and tell them what she told the doctor and have them turn their backs, too? There was just no more trust left in her.

The counselor asked her to read the names and on the paper one of the names was the name of one of the psychologists that volunteered at the Rape Crisis Center. The counselor told her that particular psychologist had excellent credentials. She hung up, called, asked for an appointment, and simply said she was depressed. The secretary said they had an appointment open at three o'clock that day, but she

J.L. Pitts

felt she couldn't say anything coherent to anybody else that day so she got an appointment for the next day. She went to her room, got the gun, and sat down on the bed with the gun on her lap. There was only the void swirling before her. She thought of nothing or no one else -- she was completely alone with the void and the gun. Voices in her head said, "You can go now, you have too much pain out there, but in here there is no pain." She knew if she pulled the trigger God would find her in the void and take her home. It was so nice in the void, no pain, and no heartaches -- just quiet calm darkness. The voices said, "You will find God here, He will take you in his arms again just like when you were nine, He will give you peace, you have suffered enough."

The words sounded so right. They sounded so true. But she had not slept in so long and she was so tired by then. She needed to sleep and with that last thought she fell asleep.- Then God sent her back from the void.

Chapter Fifteen

She awakened late after the noonday sun was at its high point in the sky. She realized she needed to bathe. How long had it been since she had bathed? She felt dirty and slimy, but didn't know if her body really felt that way or if her mind had sentenced her to that place inside herself where nothing seemed to have any cleanliness to it. She bathed, letting her naturally strawberry blond, curly hair just dry into its usual fountain of curls. She was physically ready. But mentally she couldn't possibly get in that truck and drive into Killeen and see someone to whom she would have to tell the story again. There was no story anymore -- really she did not even remember the story or what had made her so upset. She just remembered facts.

She got her things and went to the therapist's office. The waiting room was small. A dark wooden desk that looked like it could be in any office and the two comfortable chairs in front of it seemed to make the room more business-like even for its size. She sat on a love seat against the wall and looked down a hallway that seemed like it went on forever. In her mind she was thinking *that* is where the psychologist had her sessions. She deduced this by the fact that the door to one office on the other side was dark and had the door open. The other two doors in the hall were restrooms. But down at the end of the hall there was a closed door with light showing through the door jamb. Then suddenly it came open and out walked a petite woman with glasses soothing a tearful woman as they came down the hall together. She steeled herself! No one would see her cry! Not even that Army doctor had seen her cry! He had just seen her hysterical but no one was going to see her like that anymore either.

The psychologist introduced herself and she told the petite woman with glasses and deep blue eyes what her first name was. They walked down the hallway that seemed to go on forever and entered an office that was more like an apartment. It had two love seats facing each other and even though they were different pieces they complimented each other. There was also an overstuffed chair at the end of them and together the furniture formed a U pattern. She sat down on the love seat by the wall and just knew the psychologist would sit in the overstuffed chair to seem more like the focal point of the room. She watched the psychologist sit right across from her on the other love seat. Then the petite woman with glasses, deep blue eyes, and caring face asked her about herself.

She immediately started by telling the psychologist that she had been raped at 16 and immediately the psychologist stopped her with words that impacted her life forever from that day forward. The woman simply stated, "I asked you to tell me about yourself not what happened to you."

It stopped her in mid-sentence. "Well, she thought, "who am I?" She stammered out that she was an army wife and felt that would say it all.

But the petite woman with glasses, deep blue eyes, short brown hair and caring face asked, "What are some of your hobbies?" She really had none to tell but she looked around the room and saw a lot of books on shelves, which reminded her she liked to read, so that was what she told the psychologist. "Is there anything else?" The psychologist asked her. She said she did not know of anything and she did not tell the psychologist that she barely even read anymore. That most of her time was spent watching late night television and sleeping as long as she could until her husband came back home from work. The psychologist would probably think she was a loser. Then it was time to end the appointment. She realized that for most of the appointment she had been taking in the room with all its nooks and crannies. She had looked at everything in the office at least once and the answering of questions had been like awakenings to where she actually was and what she was actually doing. But she was dry eyed when she came down what seemed now to be a short hallway. She sat in one of the chairs in front of the desk and the psychologist automatically made another appointment for a week later.

Her husband came home from field maneuvers a day after she had met the psychologist. She did not dare tell him about the void and the gun. But she did tell him about the breakdown and the Army doctor and how he was so cold and calloused. She told him about the hotline and how they helped her find the psychologist and that she had an appointment to see her again in a few days. He told her that he knew that she had been at a breaking point but that he had hoped he would be home when it happened.

She asked him why he thought she would break down and he told her it was little things, like he knew she was afraid to leave the house without him. He knew when they went to the commissary to buy groceries she would flee the crowds and the store and let him stand in line to actually buy the food. He said her eyes would get big with fright if he asked her to stay and he said he knew he could not stand to see her look so terrified. So he always just let her go to the car. He told her that she did it at the Post Exchange, also. He said they would have a buggy full of things they needed but if the lines were too long that she would just leave the buggy and go home. Then there was the fact that she stayed up all night to see him off in the morning, then sleep a few hours and get back up, but would never really rest.

She was astonished that everything he had said was true. But she had not realized she had been doing those very things until he blatantly pointed them out to her. He said he knew it was coming and he was afraid he would not be there for her when it happened. He had been right. He asked her all about the psychologist and what it was like. She gave him a detailed description of the office, the secretary, and the psychologist. He said he was proud of her for doing it all by herself and that he thought it would help a lot. Again she left out the void and the gun.

They did all the normal things they would do after he had a field maneuver. She washed his dirty uniforms and sleeping bag and cleaned his gear for the next maneuver. She was so happy her Knight was home. She hardly noticed how the days flew by and it was the day for her next appointment. She just knew this was the day the psychologist would try to *break* her so she brought her Knight with her. The psychologist asked her to come down the short hallway. The woman spied her husband sitting and waiting for her to come back out. The psychologist asked him if he would like to join them and since it was the day she thought the psychologist would try to break her she agreed he should come, too.

She sat on the same loveseat that she had before and studied the room as her husband sat down beside her. They held hands. Her grip on his hand was a little tighter than his was on hers. The psychologist extended her hand to shake his hand and introduced herself. Her husband and the psychologist talked a long time about her and why he thought his wife was hurting so bad. He started talking about some of the things he had seen with his own eyes, like the way her family treated her even as an adult. She heard them talking, and listened to him as he answered the psychologist's questions and asked questions right back. She listened quite intently as she scanned the room and interjected when she felt that it was her turn to say things that would answer not only her Knight's questions but would answer her own. The psychologist said one last thing and purposefully turned to face him. "This will be a long journey for you both but especially for your wife. There may be times that she wants to share everything and there will be times when she closes herself off to everyone, even you. Just remember it is a coping mechanism she uses to keep herself safe after years of feeling unsafe."

Chapter Sixteen

The psychologist focused her first sessions on her life as an Army wife. She was happy about that because there were good things to tell her. The miscarriages came up and that was awful to talk about. She told the psychologist how since she was little she had wanted to not only be a mama but a *good mama* at that. She was highly intelligent and her school counselors made her take College Bound classes instead of classes like Sewing or Home Economics. She was not even able to take Home Health Aide. The counselors kept pushing her into advanced classes and were not taking her own dream, to be a mother one day, into consideration. She just kept doing as they told her and made above average grades except in Math. She had barely held on to a C in Math. She looked back at all these classes and the only ones she liked were Biology and Spanish as a Second Language. That was because the teachers in those classes really loved what they taught. In her junior year, she had taken Biology II as an elective class, but she could only go to school half a day. Her mother had put her in the Work as You Learn Program for the other half of the day that netted her that great, headed-for-college, burger joint job. Her mother insisted she be in the program so every day after school she worked a shift and she worked longer shifts on the weekend. It was all under a contract with the school that she did not work morning shifts or after nine o'clock on school nights, but they could work her every day. On the weekends she was at their mercy. She had a job before this one -- taking care of three small precious girls -- and that was where she shined. But her mother wanted her to get a *real* job and take care of her own needs. This had gone on for about six months and she only got to babysit the girls when she had time off. Then the burger joint was bought out. That meant all the school contracts were null and void and so she had worked longer shifts and every weekend. That had gone on for about another month and eventually they had made the error of giving her the three-to-eleven shift during a weeknight. She called her mom when she got her schedule that week and told her that they wanted her to do the closing shift. When she got home she showed it to her mother so she could see for herself what was scheduled. Her mother called and explained they could only work her until nine o'clock at night because of the contract that she had with the school. The supervisor told her mother she would be fired if she did not work the shift and to her own astonishment and amazement her mother told them that her daughter would not be coming in that night or any more nights because as far as she was concerned, her daughter was no longer working for them. She had felt so much love for her mother at that moment. There had been three managers and every time one would see her doing something he would switch her into another position. Finally one day it had all come to a head and she got all the managers together and told them she was a good worker but could not do what all of them wanted at one time. They needed to make up their minds as to what they wanted her to do and in the meantime she was going to wash dishes. It was the first time she had ever stood up for herself. After what her mother had done, she was free of them! Her mother had stood up for her and she would not have to deal with those three stooges anymore! She called the lady she babysat for and asked her for her old job back. The lady was so surprised and happy but she told her she could only pay her the same wages but would give her car privileges and provide her with money to take the kids on outings on the weekend and in the summer. She told the psychologist that the babysitting job had been the one that made her the happiest because it fulfilled her motherly instincts.

That is how the sessions went with the psychologist, who wanted to learn about the everyday times of her life as a teen and young child. The time was coming for deeper conversations and she knew it, but so far she had only told the psychologist about the good things that had happened in her life. One day the psychologist asked her to draw a picture of her family. She liked the sound of that and she was able to choose from crayons, pencils and pens. She picked up a black crayon and drew her husband and herself. The psychologist said, "Look at the picture and tell me about what you see."

"Well," she said, "the tall one with the short hair and mustache is my husband and the smaller one with curly hair is me."

The psychologist asked, "Could that be because you feel he is the biggest person in your house, the most important?" She readily agreed. Yes, he was more important. "What else do you see?" The psychologist asked. She mentioned that they were holding hands. But the psychologist pointed out that only her husband had hands and feet: the drawing she had made of herself had no hands or no feet either. The psychologist pointed out someone with no hands and no feet could not take care of themselves and would not be able to get away from danger. Then it was time. Her hour was up and the drawing was still in front of her as she asked the psychologist what it meant. All the psychologist would say was that she wanted her to go home and think about the picture. How she could not do anything for herself and how could she ever get away from danger if she did not have her own hands and feet?

She left the psychologist's office, stopped and paid her bill, and went out to sit in her car. The whole time she was driving home she thought about that picture. Once there she made lunch and thought more about the drawing she had made. Of course her Knight would be bigger than her because he made sure she was safe. He had to have hands and feet to be able to protect her. What still bothered her the most was that she had no feet and no hands. She thought about the drawing more through that week and tried to rationalize why she did not have hands and feet. She then remembered that their hands were interlinked. Maybe she did not have a hand, but he was holding onto her and was keeping her right beside him to protect her.

When it was time for her appointment with the psychologist she felt like she knew the answer. She walked down what seemed to be a very long hallway and into the room. She saw the picture was there on the table, ready for her to talk about. She knew the simple answer and told the psychologist that her husband was her Knight in shining armor. He was bigger and had hands and feet because he led the way. She felt satisfied with the answer. The psychologist asked, "How could a knight lead a person with no feet and no hands anywhere? He would not be able to lead you. He would have to carry you." The psychologist continued, "I am sad for the Knight. What a load he must bear."

She asked the psychologist, "Why don't I have hands and feet?"

The psychologist replied, "Maybe you never grew them. Maybe you came from your parent's house right into your husband's house and never had the chance to grow any hands and feet." But that could not be," she said. She had taken care of the three little girls and so surely she had hands and feet.

The psychologist said, "The answer to that is the mother gave you the hands and feet she had for her children for you to borrow while she was gone."

She sat there, looked at the picture, and asked, "Then where are my hands and feet?" The psychologist suggested she never grew them. "But everyone had hands and feet -- why would I be the only one not to have them?"

The psychologist answered, "A lot of my clients do not have hands and feet." That made her a little more at ease. Oh, so not everybody had hands and feet! "No," the psychologist said, "Not everyone had hands and feet and there is always a reason behind it."

"-What is the reason?" she asked, thinking it would be the same answer for her as it was for them. To her dismay the psychologist said that every reason was different for each person. She hated the stupid picture! It was just a picture! She had just forgotten to draw in the hands and feet! It didn't mean anything anyway! But her mind cried out, *"What does it mean?"* The time was up and the psychologist said to her, "I have a book I would like you to read. It's about boundaries, where one person starts and the other person ends."

She took the book home and started reading it. First of all, she had the right to say "No!" All those times she did not want to do something that someone had asked her to do and she had done it anyway had been in order for her to keep the friendship. That was just not right! It meant that the relationship was not healthy. She should be able to say no to things people asked of her and not be afraid of losing her friends over it. Reading that was an emotional moment for her. How many times had she done things she had not liked because she felt she could not say no because it might make her lose that friend? How many times had she said yes to her husband instead of no in fear he would leave her? The book was saying she had a right to say no. She had never learned to say no. Not in all her life. She had always told everyone yes even when she was afraid to do what they asked.

Memories flooded her head that week -- sad, sick, haunting memories. She called and made her appointment two days earlier than for when it had originally been scheduled. She wanted to tell the psychologist all the things she had said, "Yes" to or had not said, "No" to in her life. How it was just sickening what she had let herself do just because she was afraid to say, "NO!". That she remembered her mother being beaten by her father: beaten and beaten over and over in one night and her mother screamed "No!" the whole time and it did not help anything anyway. "No" had no strength in her world anyway.

101

Chapter Seventeen

Before she had her next meeting with the psychologist, so many sickening memories had been inside her head floating around that she was close to going to the void again. She stood at the edge and wondered if with all these new memories if she just should jump in. She decided instead to see the psychologist. She would not cry, she would not sniffle -- she would just be as strong as she could.

The psychologist could see there was something wrong right away and asked what had happened to make her so upset. She replied in a dead pan voice, "I read the book." The psychologist asked her what part had her so upset. She just said in the same voice with a blank looking stare, "I could have said no."

"When could you have said no?" The psychologist asked.

She responded with the blank stare and a crackling throat, "All my life I could have said no."

The psychologist looked at her, smiled a sad smile, and shook her head. "You did not know you had the right to say no until you read that book. Is that correct?"

She thought about that statement and it sounded right, but how could it be right? When a person is a child, he or she is always taught to say "Yes". When a child starts saying "No" he or she is about the age of two. At that age grown-ups start re-enforcing the word "yes". "Yes you *will* pick up your toys! Yes you *will* eat everything on your plate!" The word "no" is taught to be a thing children do not say to a grown up or even someone older than them. It's about power and unfortunately there are some people who take advantage of children that have learned to say "yes" or even the ones who cannot say anything at all. The memory she had in the airport about the friend of her sisters that told her to play baby and act like she was breastfeeding and to suck her breast came flooding into her thoughts. That girl was not a grown up and she had not told that girl "No". Ashamedly she related the story of the girl and said right then she could have said "No".

The psychologist looked at her square in the face and said, "They were telling you that you could play with them finally if you did what they said. They had more power than you did. You were just a little child while they were older children and they had been sexualized already. They were doing to you what had been done to them it was a learned behavior. Just like wanting to be a part of something and not always be the outsider led you to participate by not saying "No", but their behavior was learned from older adults and both behaviors by the adults and by those older children were out of line and stole your innocence."

She looked back at the psychologist and said, "But I did not *have* to do it."

"Right," the psychologist said. "You did not *have* to do it but you were a very small child put into a grown up situation. Like any other child, you just wanted to be included in the group of children that were older and it seemed if you could do what she asked then you would be accepted. There was no way when you sucked her breast that you could have known that it was from a sexual need she had. You did not even

know what sex meant."
Oh, how she wanted to believe those words. She thought of other times she wished she had said "No" and realized there had always been more power over her than what the child in her was capable of handling. So she did not say "No" because the powers over her led her into believing that it was a thing she could do to be more grown-up. She never really had the chance to say "No". Most of the memories were of things secretly being done to her. Like the night with the moaning man. She was so scared there was no way she could do anything but freeze.

She had been talking aloud and did not realize how many secrets she was revealing. The psychologist had been listening very intently to her way of trying to reconcile the realization that there had been no chance to say "No". She was either emotionally bullied into whatever it was or had been forced by someone with more power over her than she had. She had reacted the ways she had in order for her to keep herself safe. Memories flew through her head. In each situation, she could see what the psychologist had said was right. Even with that knowledge she looked at the psychologist and said she still felt sick because she had done those things.

The psychologist gave her another book and this one would change her life. It was "The Right to Innocence: Healing the Trauma of Childhood Sexual Abuse" by Beverly Engel. *The right to innocence*, what did that mean? Then it was time. The hour was over.

She paid her bill, went to her car, and thought about how the psychologist had said that she had been taught she could not say "No". She went home and made dinner like always but while she was making it, she devoured the book. She had been born innocent. No one had the right to take away that innocence. There were myths and facts about childhood sexual abuse. She read every one of them and realized she had believed every myth ever told and that not one person in her life had told her anything different. She thought of her brother and sisters -- she had some memories about them, too. They could not have known their innocence was being stolen away either. She remembered when she was five and her younger brother was three and a half. The teenage neighbor boy came over from next door and started tickling them as they were rolling in the grass. The teenager kept putting his fingers up her dress and touching things that made her feel funny. Things that made her sick and made her want to escape. She got away from him and said, "I'm not playing anymore!" but she did not think about her brother. Was he getting touched too? He had long pants and he seemed to be happy and not upset like she had been. She had just left him there and went inside the house. She knew what the neighbor had done that day was not right. She did not want to remember it but it was a part of her stolen innocence. She learned so much from that one book. The book that explained to her that as her mother and father got drunk in the bar while she and her siblings stayed in the front diner and fell asleep in booths on weekends -- yes, that had stolen her innocence too. Seeing all the beatings her mother had taken from her father -- yes that too had stolen her innocence.

It was not just about sexual abuse. It was how things were laid out, how the people in her life had opened a way for bad people with ill intentions to easily walk into her life and the lives of the other children. There had been a lot of drinking by the adults when she was little. All the adult members of her family -- mother, father, aunts, and uncles -- were all drunks back when she was little. She remembered being up in an orange tree with her younger brother and sister outside their uncle's bathroom and when they peeked in he started masturbating in front of them. *Oh My God!* She had thought. It was her uncle! It was too much!

She became numb, went to the bathroom, got the razor from the shelf, and sat down. She was in the void. There was no sound, no light, only darkness swirling around her. The voices inside her head said, *It's too much to bear! Use the razor -- you will slowly go to sleep there will not be any more pain here God will find you and you will be in His Arms of Light again just like when you were nine.* It all sounded so right, it all sounded so easy to believe. No more pain. No more torment. *No more memories!* She stayed at the edge of the void, listening to the voices in her head over and over. Before she followed them, her husband knocked at the door and God sent her back from the void.

Chapter Eighteen

She got in her car for the drive to the psychologist's office. What innocence? How could she have learned to say "No"? What boundaries? Then there *she* was! The little blond haired girl with blood on her hands looking up at her to ask what did it mean? She saw the dirty dishwater, smelled the marijuana and tasted beer in her mouth. It was just too much! Her whole life had been nothing but a series of experiences where she had been unable to say "No". The physical abuse, mental abuse, never having learned boundaries and it all led to sexual abuse. What did that little girl mean? What about the other one that was dirty and had scars all over her -- what did they mean? Were they memories of something she had seen? She was sure she had not seen any girls who looked like that in her life before!

She pulled up in front of the psychologist's office and thought, *why do I keep coming here? All these bad memories are just being dredged up and I am about to lose my mind.* She sat in the car knowing she was going to be late and the secretary could see her sitting in the car. Finally, she opened the door and went in. She felt like a bomb was going off inside her. She was shaky and could not catch her breath. She told the psychologist she felt like she needed to run away somewhere. The psychologist led her down the hallway and they sat on their love seats. The psychologist looked calm and sat back unaffected by the storm that was blistering inside her. She however,

J.L. Pitts

sat on the edge of the love seat, so close to the edge she almost fell off. She had her head in her hands and was telling the psychologist she could not stand anymore of the memories or the pain.

The psychologist spoke in her calm voice and said, "Today we are going to make a safe place for you to go when you get to the edge like this. Close your eyes and see with your mind someplace peaceful." She imagined a forest around a large piece of open land. The psychologist said, "Tell me about it.

She said, "There is a forest around it and the forest has trees but no underbrush underneath the trees, just smooth grass. And inside the trees is a large spot of green grass." The psychologist told her she was making a safe place in her mind that she could go to when things got too much for her to handle. The psychologist asked her to tell her things she would put in this place that would comfort her. She said, "There would be a blanket and a picnic basket that had red and white cloth all inside it and there would be napkins to match. There would be fried chicken and potato salad and plates and silverware and in a blue cooler there would be lots of my favorite cola." The psychologist asked if she would be alone and she said yes. It was just for her.

"What about the sky?" The psychologist asked.

"Oh," she said, "It's a beautiful blue with white puffy clouds." The psychologist asked her if there was anything else that was soothing to her there. She answered, "Yes there was a cool breeze and it was a warm day." The psychologist asked her if she felt safe there and she said, "Yes."

Neither one spoke for a few moments. She created her safe place while the psychologist sat silently

watching the stress and pain drain from her face. She slowly opened her eyes and realized she was sitting comfortably on the couch. She did not feel the need to run anymore or feel that a bomb was going off inside her. The psychologist explained that they had used imagery to find a safe spot for her to go to and she could always go to her safe spot if she ever felt like this again. She asked, "Will it work every time?" It will only work if you can get to that safe place in your mind," the psychologist answered. She looked scared and the psychologist caught the look. She explained what she had was called a panic attack. She went on to explain further. "Imagery works for most people but if it doesn't work for you I can refer you to a psychiatrist that could prescribe medication."
She was stunned -- she did not need any medication! She read how people got stuck on those nerve pills and she refused to be a pill popper. The psychologist could see her unwillingness to work through this with medication. She would use imagery and guided imagery to help her get through the rough spots. Then it was time. She gathered her purse and followed the psychologist to the front desk where she paid the secretary.
She went home, laid on the bed, thought about her safe place and slept soundly for two hours. That week flew by and she just kind of stayed in her safe place most of the time if she was not doing something that kept her mind busy. When she went back for her next appointment she looked more relaxed and calm. The psychologist commented on it right away and she explained what she had been doing all week. The psychologist said she had needed that rest. She brought out the crayons, pencils and pens and said,

"Today I want you to draw me a house."
She grabbed a pen and started making a house. She made a two level house with two windows upstairs and two windows downstairs, but the windows were higher up off the ground than usual. It had a triangle roof and a chimney with smoke coming out of it. The psychologist told her the house represented her and she should be glad because it was a good house. She was asked to tell about the house and all the windows. She started explaining her house. The psychologist noticed each window had four window panes but there was not anything behind them. She just told the psychologist there were curtains over them.
The psychologist said, "So you don't want anyone looking in."
She said well, "No I don't."
The psychologist spoke again saying, "That explains why your windows are so high up off the ground. You are scared of what people will see." She was becoming ill at ease because her house was telling more about her than she believed it could. The psychologist started pointing things out. "Look at the door -- the way into your life -- your real life where you don't allow but a few to go. Your door is off the ground and there is no step to get up to it and it has a tiny doorknob but it's such a big door. Such a wide and big door says you have room for a lot of people. However, the tiny doorknob says only a really smart person could open that big door with that tiny doorknob." She was amazed this picture was telling the psychologist things she needed to be saying but did not know how to say them with her own words. Then the psychologist placed a hand on top of hers in a reassuring gesture. "The chimney is a phallic symbol."

She asked, "Do you know what that means?"

"No," she said in a small voice, thinking something big was about to be revealed.

The psychologist looked at her with those deep blue eyes and caring face and explained, "A phallic symbol was a symbol that stood for a penis."

Immediately she withdrew her hand quickly and answered, "Well you are right about most of it but not about *that!*" She had a fireplace in the house she grew up in, so her drawing a chimney meant nothing.

"Look at it again," the psychologist asked her.

She looked again. It was rectangular in shape, had a covering all around the top, and smoke was coming out of it. No! No, *that* could not be! But it was and she knew it was. "But what does it mean?"

"Well," the psychologist said, "if it was just a chimney it might symbolize the man was the head of the household. But *your* chimney has smoke coming out of it that is going a long way off into the clouds."

The psychologist asked if she could tell what that meant to her.

"No," she said, "I can't think of what that would mean." Then it was time.

The doctor said, "Think about the chimney, what it represents and how that may have affected your childhood." She paid her bill and went home with that in her head. Gratefully by the time she had driven home, she was in her safe place and she did not think of it again that week.

Chapter Nineteen

He was her Knight in shining armor! He always had been and when he got home she as always asked about his day and he would tell her all the news from his company and from the motor pool. They ate together, chatting back and forth as they enjoyed their meal. They watched television until nine o'clock and would each take a shower. They got in their nice warm waterbed, snuggled up, and went to sleep. They had not made love in a long time but they had discussed it and had both realized that with all the horrible things going on in therapy it was not a good idea to be having sex when some memory could be triggered to make her lose it! Instead they just peacefully snuggled up and that was how that week went by.

When she realized that her next appointment was on the same day as the company Family Day she called to reschedule but there was nothing available until the week after. She knew she had a doctor's appointment at the Army hospital that week and she was unsure of the day so she would have to call back.

She stayed very busy and it was not until she was at the doctor appointment that she realized it had almost been two weeks since she had been back to therapy. When she got home that afternoon she called and made an appointment for the next week. That was the week her husband would go on night maneuvers for their field training. He would not be back for another two weeks. She sighed. Being an Army wife was not easy.

The next week came and her husband went to his field exercise while she went back to therapy. She had forgotten the drawing, the chimney, the phallic symbol, but right there on the table between them was the paper. She immediately tried to find something to say about the phallic symbol and what it could mean. When she was asked had she thought about the picture in the three weeks since she had been there, She replied in all honesty that she had not.

The psychologist looked at her and said, "That is an important detail in your picture. Has something happened to you in the past that you do not feel like you could share?"

Yes, she had tried to tell the psychologist the very first day of therapy that her brother-in-law had raped her when she was almost seventeen. She repeated the story. But when she did, the little blond haired girl with the blood on her hands was in her mind, looking up at her and asking what did it mean. She had never told anybody about her visions of the two different girls. All of a sudden she told her psychologist about the little blond haired girl with the sweat on her forehead and no air was coming in from the trailer window where she sat naked on the bed.

The little girl was her.

She had never seen that girl before because she just could not be her, she just could not be that little girl. That was the first time she cried in that office. It was not just tears in her eyes -- it was brokenhearted sobs. That little blond haired girl with the blood on her hands had been her all along from when she was eleven years old.

For the first time she remembered that hot day in

spring. He had come to her mother's house and talked his usual smooth conversation with her mother. Then as he was about to leave he asked her mother if she could come with him and help clean his trailer for when her sister got home. He was the Great One. He helped mom and dad with all kinds of projects. He was the tennis pro of their county and always brought the children colas and goodies. He was upper middle class and their family was lower middle class. He seemed like a god to the children.

Her! He had picked her! She was so excited! The Great One had picked her. When she got to the trailer she had immediately gone to do the dishes. She could smell the sour dish water and saw that the water was gray all around them. *Yuck*, she thought, but knew she could do this. She was helping the Great One. She had drained the water from the sink and he had said, "Come over here. You are a big girl now. Just get comfortable." He had handed her a beer. She had felt so grown up. He had told her she was old enough to party with him a little bit. She felt even more grown up. He was rolling something in paper that looked liked mom and dad's cigarettes but smaller with no end to it -- just paper twisted at both ends. He lit it and showed her how to draw the smoke down her throat. He then asked her if she knew what a "shotgun" was. She knew her father had a shotgun but he said, "No this will be how we smoke this joint together at the same time." He put one end in her mouth, one end in his, blew real hard, and the smoke choked down her lungs.

She became dizzy right away because the beer and marijuana had been too much for her little body to take. She was soon beyond being able to think straight. But she remembered him saying, "Your mom will be real mad at you if you go home like this so you should come lay down." He took her to a small hot bedroom with only a sheet on the bed. He said, "It's too hot in here. You need to take your clothes off."

In her stupor and to please the Great One she did as she was told. She must have fallen asleep because the next thing she knew his naked body was sliding onto hers. He had her legs opened and when his chest was level with her head, she felt it. She knew what it was but did not know how to stop it. She had lain there frozen. She felt him enter her and there had been a feeling of pain as he pushed his way in and then she felt the tearing sensation. It was extremely painful but she did not cry out. She was terrified by what was happening. Time was going by but she did not think about anything but that he was hurting her. She did not make a sound because he might make the pain worse.

He got off of her and said, "Ride me." She did not know what that meant but he pulled her on top of him and as he tried to re-enter her, she begged him not to do that to her. He got up nonchalantly and said he was going to take a shower.

He left the hot room and she had sat up on the edge of the bed sweating and numb, all except for the place that was hurting so bad. There was blood coming from her body and while trying to find out from where it came and how to stop it she got blood on her hands and lifted them up to see what it meant. He came back to the room and asked her if she had started her period yet. She knew what that meant because they had seen a film in school about it but she shook her head no.

"Oh," he said. "That just means your period will come soon."

She had sat there with the blood on her hands and the pain in her body. He told her to go to the bathroom and clean up but not to take a shower or her mother would know what she had been doing.

She had cleaned as best as she could and washed the blood off her hands in the sink. The bleeding had stopped but the pain had not. She went back to the hot little bedroom and got her clothes on. She walked to the dirty smelly sink of dishes and started cleaning them because that is what he had told her mother she would be doing. He said, "We do not have time for that. I need to get you home. You cannot tell your mother or she will get very mad at you for doing things that only grown-ups should do."

She thought about the beer, that funny cigarette, and what he had done to her in the bedroom. She knew it was sex just like the film said at school. Her mother would hate her if she knew she told on the Great One and made him look bad like he really was. They would not believe her because she still sucked her thumb and wet the bed. Who would believe her over the Great One?

He had taken her outside and while he was starting the little car he looked over at her and said she should not let other boys do that to her. Anger filled her. It was her body and only *she* would choose if she ever did that again. Her head had been fuzzy, she felt weird inside her head, and still had pain down there. But he took her home.

She had walked in the house and gone straight to her bedroom to lay down on her bed. She said nothing to her mother. But the Great One told her mother what a great help she had been. Then her mother said that was surprising because as bad as her eyesight was she had to be made to do things at least twice to get things done the right way. He assured her mother that she had done just fine and he was ready for her sister to get home. She had laid on her bed, wondering when the pain would stop and why her mother had not come and checked on her. But the Great One was still talking and her mother said, "Oh she will be fine. She is just worn out from doing some real work. Do not worry about her -- she will be up and going the rest of the day when she wakes up."

She had wondered when the pain would end as she had fallen into a hard and deep sleep. She had awakened to a numb feeling throughout her body and she didn't feel any pain, anywhere, anymore. She had wanted the stench of beer and marijuana and his sweaty body off of her and even though it was early evening she went and took a hot bath to scrub his sweat and the blood off her body. She had lain in the tub of extremely hot water while it turned her skin bright red. It had been then that she made the decision that no one would ever believe if she told. She would not tell anyone and she would also not tell it to herself ever again. And another shard was broken.

Chapter Twenty

Her time was finished, but the sobbing had not subsided so the psychologist sat there very quietly and let her cry until she could cry no more. She became very still and quiet as she repeated, "It was me" over and over again. She sat up, her eyes were swollen, and she needed some tissues. "All those years of seeing her in my head, asking what the blood meant -- it had meant he stole my virginity."

Now she knew and there was nothing she could do but accept it and deal with the memory. The psychologist looked at her with real pain in those deep blue eyes. She comforted her by saying, "Now you know what that little girl was saying. Now you can take the fear out of that memory by doing what you did today -- remembering it and bringing it to the surface." She slowly rose to her feet and felt quite shaky. Again the psychologist said she could get in with the psychiatrist and he could give her some medicine to get through this time period. She refused and said, "Thank you anyway."

She walked numbly to her car. Her husband was not home because of the field training exercise and would not be back for almost two more weeks. She was all alone with a hole inside her she thought she would never be able to fill. She had friends she could call but the horrifying memory was too much to share with any of her new found friends, so she called her best friend back home and as she told the story she started sobbing all over again. And her friend said two words that shook her to the core: she said *she knew.*

But how could her friend have known? She had kept it a secret for so many years. She did not remember ever telling her friend! But late the night it had happened she had hid behind the bookcase and told her friend about the rape. She asked her best friend why she had never said anything, especially since she had revealed that she had been raped again at sixteen and her friend had known about that horrifying situation, too. Her best friend told he that she had been so devastated about what he had done when she was sixteen that she could not bring to remind her about what happened when she was eleven. Her best friend must have thought she had forgotten it somehow. Her friend kept the secret to keep her from a memory she did not want to remember.

She was stunned! Her friend, by trying to save her from pain when she was a child, had set her up for the rape that had happened at sixteen. All because her friend thought she never remembered it happening. She felt that if she had known she could have done something differently. But it was no one's fault but her own.

He got away with it once and since she did not tell he thought he could get away with it again.

She had hidden the first rape because she felt no one would believe her. That had allowed him to believe that if she did not tell the first time she never would

Her friend had kept these secrets to save her pain. That childhood friend was remembering and recanting the memories because she knew her devastated friend was finally ready to hear them. It was time to receive confirmation of the truth. Her friend had a lot of memories saved in her heart and mind because a lot of things had happened, things she herself had suppressed but vowed to face and deal with going forward.

That childhood friend had held her memories for her, had carried the load of that heartache until it was safe to remember them once more. She told her friend she loved her, but said she did not want to know anything else, then thanked her over and over for carrying the burden of those memories.

She sat down and wrote her mother a long letter to tell her of all the molestation -- what had happened to her at eleven and again at sixteen. She laid bare everything she remembered, made a copy for herself, put the original into a stamped envelope, and sent it on its way to her mother back home. Her sister had divorced the rapist since then because he had physically abused her constantly, but for some reason her mother still acted like he was the Great One. That was not only a statement, it was a living fact. Her mother still talked to his mother, to him, and let him come over even when she would be home visiting. Her mother sent her a letter back telling her she was losing it and that the psychologist must be putting things in her head. Her mother went on to say she was not going to have that kind of talk brought back to her house and that she would always speak to the father of her grandchildren. Her mother had chosen. To her it was very clear that even if she had told when she was eleven they would have swept it under the rug.

She was so thankful she never told because this way she would only have to live with the memory of the rape. She would have surely entered the void if she had told her story back then and had to live knowing her mother and father knew about it but covered it up to keep it as just another family secret.

She went to the psychologist and showed both of the letters. Her letter was about all the abuse, all the molestation, the rapes, and the alcoholic lifestyle that stole her and her siblings' innocence and the fact that her parents would leave them with practical strangers so they could go out and get drunk and what happened to her because of that. She remembered that she had only been seven and they had left them with a migrant family that they had known from orange picking days. She had wondered where they were when the twenty-something-year-old son had wanted to teach her how to French kiss. She already knew the answer: her parents had been out getting drunk.

Her psychologist gave her a new book: "Divorcing Your Family while You Heal." She took it home and read it two times by the time of her next appointment. When she took the book back she had another letter that she was going to mail but had not yet. She shared it with her psychologist first. It was a letter of divorce. It started out with how much she loved them all but ended with her saying she was divorcing them until the time she felt she was strong and safe enough to deal with their denial of the loss of her innocence. The psychologist let her cry as she put it in the envelope and sealed it.

She mailed the letter of divorce on her way home. Her husband was back and she told him everything. He was astounded she had the courage to do that! All their married life he had been there to protect her from the hurtful things her family had done and said, which most of the time was some off-handed remark that they did not even mean to say. They decided to change their phone number to an unpublished one

J.L. Pitts

and she kept on with therapy.

Chapter Twenty-One

The next week she went back to the doctor, the pencils, crayons, and pens along with a blank sheet of paper were on the table. She was told to simply draw a tree. She sat down with black, brown, and green crayons. First she took the black crayon and outlined the whole tree. Then she colored in the top of the tree with green and the bottom of the tree with brown. Then she was asked to explain what she saw in her picture She said, "Just a tree."

But the psychologist said, "Look more closely. What does it resemble?" She could not follow the line of thought the psychologist was pointing her into. It looked like it was going to end up being like the picture she drew of her house -- a symbol. But since she could not figure it out the psychologist told her what it represented.

Her tree looked like a big fist on top of a long arm. "What does it mean?" she asked.

The psychologist stated, "It means you're angry."

"Yes, I am angry," she said out loud. She was told to look what she had done to the fist. She had closed it up in an outline of black. The psychologist started explaining that she was still not getting to the core of her anger. That she always kept it within the normal lines. She had to ask what that meant *being inside the normal lines*.

The psychologist started asking her questions about being angry. "What do you feel like when you get angry?" She said she felt tight in her skin and that she should not be angry because it only led to bad things. The psychologist said, "Everyone gets angry and it does not have to always lead into bad things. What bad things did anger lead you into when you were a child?"

In her childhood home she had been punished for anger. She had always been taught she had no right to get angry with her parents -- they were right and she was wrong. The psychologist asked her what would happen if she showed anger to her mother or father. She knew the answer to that right away: she would be whipped with a belt. The psychologist then asked what would happen if her siblings got angry with her. She remembered that they would usually yell, curse, or call her bad names and if it got physical she would just run away most of the time, except when she had a fight with her older brother. He would track her down and beat her up. The psychologist asked, "When he beat you up, did you ever tell your mother?"

"Yes," she said. Once she had asked her mother to make him stop, but her mother's only words of advice were go back out there and kick his butt.

The psychologist's questions got deeper. "What about when your mother and father would fight?"

"Oh, it was bad" she told the psychologist. Her father always beat up her mother if they got in a fight. Usually it only happened when they were drunk. The psychologist asked her to look at her tree again. When she did, she saw what the psychologist was seeing: if the tree stood for anger then outlining it in black kept it contained. She then had the realization she kept her anger inside because she thought if she got angry with someone, then one or both of them would get hurt.

The next question startled her. "Have you ever gotten angry with someone for the littlest thing and it turned into a major explosion of anger?"

Yes – she answered that she had that happen a couple of times. The psychologist explained her anger was like a powder keg: when it was in the barrel left all alone it was fine, but when she finally let her anger spark it then lit the powder keg and boom -- everything she was ever mad about came down on that one person that had just made a spark too close to the powder keg. Sparks are harmless unless they are near a powder keg, then they are very dangerous things. It might take only one good spark on a short fuse to ignite the powder keg of anger inside her. Or sometimes a few sparks would have to get the fuse going to get the "boom" effect. She did not have to run away from sparks or explode from them. She was allowed to be angry about things but just not to do needless harm to others.

She sat and thought about what had just been revealed to her. It was so true. If she was mad at one of her friends, she always either stayed away from them altogether until the anger could subside or went off on them like a bomb exploding. She asked the psychologist how she could learn to *just be angry.*

The next comment made her sad. "You learn each time you get angry what the amount of anger should be allotted for that circumstance," the psychologist answered.

It would mean she had to stop, think, and then react when she got angry. She would have to do this every time before the process could become a learned behavior. She had learned how to react to anger growing up in an alcoholic household. Sometimes when she was little, she could feel the anger rising like it was a temperature that heated the air around her. She had learned by her mother's example that when you knew anger was coming, you should run and hide. They ran a lot from her father's anger. When he got drunk he usually became violent. If they did not run away from his anger she would most likely see him beat her mother. Since it had taken years learning how to survive that abuse, it would take a long time actively stopping the cycle. She had to deal with her anger before it got to the "run away" or "powder keg" stage of anger. Then it was time.

She paid her bill and went to her car. Anger had always been around her all her life. Now she was in her mid-twenties and was finally going to have to learn how to deal with it. She drove home, remembering things like when her older brother would beat her up if she did not play whatever game he wanted to play. She thought about the day she had begged her mother to make her older brother stop beating her up. All her mother had said to her was to go back out there and kick his butt. That was one of her mother's remedies for violence: try to fight back. As a witness to her own mother's abuse, she knew the woman never won by fighting back. That day she chose the other option she had been taught. She ran and hid instead of fighting him. When her father was on a drunken rampage, her mother would load her and her siblings into the car and they would go find a place to hide. Her mother wouldn't go back near him until he had sobered up, calmed down, and she felt safe he would not hurt her. She shared all those terrifying moments with her husband then thanked him for never being violent towards her. He just said he knew how scared she got if he raised his voice, so he never did. If he had a problem with her he would talk logically until things were worked out.

She had never been scared that her Knight would hit her. As a married woman she never had to run away to another person's house, never had to sleep in a car hidden in an orange grove, and never had to go to sleep in fear that he would come home drunk and beat her up. Her Knight had never shot off a shotgun in the house to make her think he was going on a killing rampage, but her father had. She remembered that night vividly! Her father came home late one Friday night from the bars, which usually meant he had probably drunk away his paycheck. She heard the start of a verbal argument through the wall of her bedroom that joined her parent's room. She knew it would become violent and she readied herself for the fight to begin. But what happened that night no child could have prepared for. That night she heard her mother say "no don't" and then heard the sound of a twelve-gauge shotgun going off and the buckshot falling on her and her siblings heads. They were all wide awake and ready to run! She remembered the house had been eerily quiet after that first blast. Then another shotgun blast came through the wall and more buckshot fell on them. She had been so terrified but she had to do something to help get the younger kids to safety. She sent the little kids to the playhouse in the trees to hide there. She also told them if their father came outside to run away from him. She had stood there not knowing if her mother was dead or alive. If he had killed their mother would he come after them? She had been astounded when all that happened was that her mother had come out of their bedroom saying, "I am taking your Daddy to the hospital." She had never once checked on the children. Her parents got in the car, left them behind, and disappeared into the night. She had gotten the little ones back in their beds but they would never sleep soundly the way a child should sleep, ever again. Her mother was soon back, saying he would stay in the hospital until they could help him get over his depression. While in the hospital they had discovered her father was bipolar and had given him medicine that changed all of their lives permanently, forever, for the good. But nothing could erase the damage his undetected illness had done to their family. Powder keg anger, yes -- she knew about that kind of anger. She realized all her anger had a border to go through to get released because she had never thought it was okay to be angry. It was just too dangerous to get angry.

Chapter Twenty-Two

Food was her comforter, so she began to eat a lot. She was already two hundred and twenty-six pounds. The emotional effect on her attempt to rid her soul of the demons of the past made eating her only comforter, especially when her husband was on field maneuvers. She had her friends that she saw regularly but never told them anything about her therapy or her past. She thought she would be cast out of the group for being a different kind of creature that none of them knew. She went to her sessions with the psychologist and learned a little more about the secrets that she had kept from herself for many years. One day she was told in a therapy session to draw a picture of her family as if she was a child. She drew her mother, father, and her four sisters, and her two brothers. Their ages ranged from the eldest at seventeen to the youngest at about two years old. The psychologist pointed to one of her siblings and asked, "Who is this?"

She quickly answered, "That's my older brother."

The psychologist asked, "Why did you draw him without a face?" It stopped her in her tracks. She was told it was not a mistake and that there was something about her older brother she did not want to see. She told the psychologist it was probably because he beat her up a lot and her mother would not do anything about it. The psychologist asked, "Then why does the mother have a face?" She said she did not know, but a feeling that something dreadful was coming hit her heart and she felt sick. Then it was time.

She went to the front desk, paid the secretary and as she left she heard the door lock behind her. She still had that dreadful sick feeling when she took off in the truck on her way to her friend's house. She was on the interstate and only had four exits to go, but at the first exit she smelled pigs and heard their grunting. At the second exit she could see her older brother laughing and eating candy out of a bag. By the third exit, a numbness started at the back of her head, flooded over her face, and enveloped her entire body. She pulled the truck off the interstate because she could not drive any further.

The memory that had been hidden inside her mind for so long was then released. Her brother had found her diary. It talked about things she would never say to any of her family and never to anyone outside the family -- all the things she wanted to say if she could. It talked about the molestation at nine and the rape at eleven, how her father and mother were drunks, that her father would beat her mother, and how much she hated her mother when she would load them up and they would have to run and hide. She had filled the entire book with the secrets of her heart, mind, body, and soul. She had buried it in a tin box underneath an old oak tree. He had it in his hands now and said she would do exactly as he said or he would give the diary to her mother and father. She had felt bile rise in her stomach, but she stayed silent as a mouse. "Get up there on the top box in the barn," he had demanded. She was afraid of what he was going to do. But she did as he commanded because no one could know the things she had written in that book. He pulled her shorts and panties down and told the friend he had with him to get up on the box so he could stick his penis in her. He then took a bag from the boy. She realized her brother had used blackmail and sold her to the boy for a bag of candy. She smelled the pigs because their pen was beside the stacked up boxes. The smell, the hot summer day, the pigs grunting, her older brother laughing and eating the candy with her diary open before him: she had locked it all in her mind so tight, so deep, that she had never thought of that memory again. Yes, she had smelled the pigs before, heard their grunting and each time she would get sick with horror but she never allowed herself to know why it had such an effect on her. Her life was nothing but one long big horror story. People had used her for their own purposes and she felt worthless enough to believe that no one would believe her so she never told. That memory had been released. She remembered every detail of that day. She had stood over the burn barrel and watched every precious private thought go up in flame one page at a time. She had gone completely numb as her mind fell apart like the pages of the diary as they burned. Another shard was broken. She had written down all the anger she had at her parents, about all the sexual abuse she had been through, and even the family secrets but the beating she would have been given and the sickened looks from her parents and siblings would have been better than what her older brother had just forced her to do. She vowed to never write again and as long as she lived in that house, she never did. The thoughts she had put down in the diary that had kept her mind from splintering burned into a blackened memory in her mind that day. Now after all these years she was on the side of the interstate, remembering it all. She

J.L. Pitts

did not know what to do with all the emotions flooding her mind. Hers was the last appointment of the day so she could not go back to get help from the psychologist. She was not capable of meeting her husband at their friend's house and having dinner with them.

The void came ... *Just lay down your troubles in here ... there is peace here ... no more pain ... no more bad memories ... you will find God in here ... just slam the truck full force against the concrete embankment ... no more memories ... no more pain ... God will find you here and give you rest just like he did when you were nine years old.* She revved the engine: she would do it this time. There would be pain when she hit the concrete embankment, but after that she would be in the void. A knock on her window scared her back to reality. It was a soldier playing the "hero." He wanted to know if she was okay, if he could help in some way. Her face was red with tears streaming down her cheeks even as she told the soldier she was fine.

"Are you sure?" he asked and again and she assured him she was fine and that she had gotten something in her eyes but had finally gotten it out. She did not know that while she was in the void she was screaming and trying to pull her hair off her head. The soldier told her what he had seen her doing and again asked her if she was really okay. She assured him this time by saying that she had just received some bad news and she would be fine. She felt herself going numb again as her tears dried up. She could even feel the numbness in her mouth. The numbness covered her up and protected her from any more feelings. He asked one more time if she was okay and if he could drive her somewhere. She assured him again and thanked him for stopping. Finally he went back to his car.

She buried the memory deep in her mind and would not think of it anymore until she could see her psychologist again. She cleaned herself up at a gas station and went to meet her husband at their friend's house. They ate dinner, went home, got in bed, and she curled up in the fetal position and went to sleep immediately. But there were dreams that tore into her brain, like seeing the book burning, smelling the pigs, and hearing their grunts, but her mind safely blocked out where all that had come from.

When her next appointment came around, she numbly she sat down, let go of the barriers, and the story rushed out of her like a dam had been broken. Her eyes burned with tears that seemed to have no end. She was given a tissue for her nose that had started running along with the tears. She said all of it without any emotion. She hoped she would never feel anything ever again but knew all the while she would have to in order to heal.

Chapter Twenty-Three

The psychologist told her it was time for a rest from therapy. That it was time for her to see other women who were struggling, trying to keep sane, and make it out of bad situations. She was told that the rape crisis center was also a battered woman's shelter. They needed someone to keep the children while the mothers went to group therapy. Her eyes brightened because that was exactly what she needed -- to help children going through hard times, which would feed her motherly instinct.

There were two group meetings, one on Tuesday night and the other on Thursday night. She went to the room and waited on the children, then introduced herself to each mother and child and asked the children if they would like to color or play. All the children, except one, chose one or the other. The one who would not choose either activity, was a blond haired, blue-eyed girl who looked to be about seven. She stood by the door like a sentry every week for both nights while the little girl's mom had therapy. She talked sweetly to the girl and told her she was safe with the other children.

Every week she talked to the girl and one day the girl came close and asked to rock with her. She had a rocking chair for herself. All the other seats were for the little ones. She felt honored. She picked the little girl up, put her on her lap, and the little girl melted into her as she sat watching the other children play among themselves. She realized what a leap of faith the little girl had taken by finally trusting her. She rocked her back and forth and hummed a Christian hymn that she had learned as a little girl and it soothed the child in her lap. And it soothed the child in her own soul. When the mothers came to pick the children up, the mother of the little girl on her lap was astounded. The mother said that her daughter had not responded to anyone in a long time. The child slid off her lap, grabbed her mother's hand, and left the room.

The shelter housed ten women and sixteen children that had been brought to the safe house in patrol cars by police officers. That was the only way they could come to the safe house, because it was just that -- a safe house. The building did not have a name or an address to it. They tried not to ever turn a woman away. They helped set up new lives for the women, helped get them into low income housing, and helped them gather all the information they would need to start a new life. Only twelve percent of them ever made it to the housing stage because they would start remembering all the good times they had had with their husbands or boyfriends and end up going back to them because they thought it would work itself out. A lot of them came back within a month and her psychologist, who handled the therapy for the women, told her it took eight to twelve times of leaving the abuser before a woman either got away from the abuse, learned to live with it, or died from it.

One night the little girl and her mother did not show up. She missed rocking the child and hoped that the mother had gotten out of her own abusive circumstances. While she volunteered there she never saw either of them again but since all cases were private she would never learn what had happened to that mother and child. She kept a place open in her heart and hoped she had made it out.

. At Christmas she finally stepped down as a volunteer and went back to therapy. She had not talked to her family of origin in the two years of therapy she had been through. So far they had only sent her letters that she never opened. She just wrote "return to sender" before she dropped them back in the mail box.

She had changed her telephone number and there was no way of finding her except through her husband's unit. The captain in charge got a call from her mother about six months after she had broken all contact. He had brought her husband before him and told him to have his wife call her mother. Her Knight told the captain that it was under her psychologist's advice to no longer have contact with her birth family. The captain said he understood and her Knight was never asked to come to the captain's office anymore on that subject.

She went back in therapy and asked her psychologist about contacting her birth family. She had been able to stay away that long because another relative that she trusted would give her updates on her family at regular intervals. The question was turned around and re-directed back to her. Her psychologist asked, Are you sure you want to make contact with your family now?"

She said, "Yes, I think I am ready." She sent a letter to tell them about what she had learned in therapy and that she had to maintain boundaries but if they wanted to talk to her to just call the new number she had written at the bottom of the letter.

The psychologist told her she was doing well and that there were now group therapy sessions for women who had been abused as children and asked her if would she like to join. She was hesitant because she thought all those women would be looking at how fat she was and would not really be listening to her. They would probably talk about her behind her back. She did not go at first but finally the psychologist asked what was keeping her from coming to the group. She told the psychologist her fears and was told that no one would make fun of her for any reason. The psychologist went on to share that it was a safe place for everyone that went there, the next session was the next evening, and she should put away feelings of unworthiness to join the group. All the women in the group were learning that there were others who had similar stories to share.

She went to the group on Monday and Wednesday but spoke very little. She listened intently and learned that some of the women had been abused beyond her comprehension and were working, living, maintaining a normal life. Some of them had known less abuse but it had stunted them in their tracks. She realized she had been stunted in her tracks as well.

One day she opened up, but all she could say was that she had lost her education. She had been in twelfth grade when she finally got away from her abusers. She felt that was the last thing the abusers stole from her. Suddenly everyone was talking at once, telling her about colleges that allowed a person to get a high school diploma and take college courses at the same time. They talked about things such as night school classes for her G.E.D., a quiet, calm, and smiling woman who was big like her told her about homeschooling. That was the first time the woman had spoken directly to her and she felt an instant bond. The woman had long thin brown hair and was a bit bigger than she herself was at that time. All she really knew was that the woman was soft spoken and like all the women in the group had been sexually abused as a child. The new-found friend stopped her after group and gave her a piece of paper with a number on it that looked like it had been hastily written. The woman gave her name again, said she could call any time, and they could get together. The woman mentioned having all the homeschooling information if she wanted it. It was the beginning of the healthiest friendship she ever had.

That night her mother called and said how much she had missed her, how much she loved her, and asked if would she come home soon and visit. She did not let on that she was crying as they talked and she was brought up to date on everyone's lives. Some of it was good news while some of it not so good. She told her mother that she loved her and missed her, but she had learned about the abuse she had been through all during her childhood and she had boundaries about those instances. Her mother said, "Sure honey, we will work it all out." She called her new friend and told her what had happened. Her friend encouraged her to go slow and keep her boundaries up. They made a date to have coffee at the new friend's home. Their friendship was sealed with good boundaries and the ability to be honest with one another.

With her new friend's encouragement she home schooled her last year of high school and got her diploma. Her friend had asthma and since she smoked, she always went outside. One day she came to her faithful friend's house and there was a bench and ashtray put on the patio especially for her to have a place to smoke. It touched her heart that even though her friend had asthma she was willing to make a special place for her to rest and smoke. She was so touched by it she called her husband at home and told him to get all smoking stuff out of the house -- lighters, ashtrays, and cigarettes -- because she was never smoking again. She never did to honor the friend who would make a new boundary just for her.

Group got better for her since she had a strong friend there to back her up. She talked about abuse that she had already remembered and sometimes new memories that would shake the very foundation she had made, but during those times she stood strong. The day after she got her diploma she had group therapy and shared her good news. She told the group that not only had she graduated high school but she felt strong enough to "graduate" from group. There were happy congratulations and sad good-byes. Her psychologist said she would still have more private sessions and that was how she left the group.

EPILOGUE

She did go to a few more sessions with her psychologist. She made pictures of a happy couple -- all with hands, feet, and clothes on them, not just stick figures anymore. She drew a house with a swing set, a cat in the yard with flagstones leading up to it, and a wide welcome mat right where the door joined the ground floor. Her windows had drawn back curtains and through the windows you could see tables, lamps, and bookshelves. She was told that she was still carefully letting people in her new life because she used flagstones instead of a path. But that was a good thing since she had just learned boundaries.

Her tree included branches and individual leaves that revealed her new strong self. This tree was different because she had created different avenues for anger to flow as signified by the flow of the tree's limbs and leaves.

The last thing she had to draw was where she felt she was right there at that point in time. She took a pencil, a red crayon, and carefully drew a woman in jeans and a shirt on a red motorcycle. Her psychologist asked, "What does it mean to you?" She explained it meant she was going forward in her life and she knew it would be an adventure from now on as she continued to learn about boundaries, limits, and new horizons. The psychologist agreed that was a very good way to look at it. She was off to new adventures and did very well ... Until the people fell out of her head ...

But that is a different part of her journey: the part with the brightest star and the darkest days.

Some details of the characters, times and/or places have been altered to protect what innocence remains

J.L. Pitts

for my family and friends.

You can contact Author J.L. Pitts at:
authorjlpitts@yahoo.com
or visit her websites:
http://authorjlpitts.wix.com/authorjlpitts
http://authorjlpitts.wordpress.com
http://www.publishwithcfa.com/j.-l.-pitts.html
https://www.facebook.com/julielambethpitts
https://twitter.com/DeborahJudges2
https://plus.google.com/+JuliePittsauthor2014/posts

Made in the USA
Middletown, DE
01 March 2015